Planning for
Recreation and Parks Facilities:
Predesign Process, Principles, and Strategies

Planning for
Recreation and Parks Facilities:
Predesign Process, Principles, and Strategies

by Jack Harper

Venture Publishing, Inc.
State College, Pennsylvania

Production Manager: Richard Yocum
Manuscript Editing: George Lauer
Photography: Dan Harper (http://www.danharperphoto.com/)

Library of Congress Catalogue Card Number: 2009926130
ISBN-10: 1-892132-85-0
ISBN-13: 978-1-892132-85-7

Table of Contents

ABOUT THE AUTHOR

JACK A. HARPER, B.Sc., M.Sc.

Jack Harper has over 37 years' experience in recreation planning and management. He was a Professor and Coordinator of Recreation Management and Community Development at the University of Manitoba from 1983 to 2007. Previously, he was a partner in Professional Environmental Recreation Consultants Ltd. (PERC), a firm specializing in recreation planning, and spent eight years in senior management with the City of Winnipeg, Parks and Recreation Department.

He is a past president of the Canadian Parks and Recreation Association and is acknowledged as a leader in the benefits of recreation movement in Canada. As a consultant, Mr. Harper has successfully completed over 70 planning projects related to sport, recreation, culture, and the entertainment industry for all levels of government, business, and the voluntary sector. His consulting work has included large-scale facility feasibility studies, major event management, economic impact assessment, organizational evaluation, strategic and business planning, public consultation strategies, economic impact assessment, and survey research.

Now retired from the University, he serves as an advisor and consultant to community groups across Canada.

Acknowledgements

Over the forty years that I have been involved in recreation and community development, I have been inspired by many great friends and colleagues who have served as teachers, mentors, and advisors. I would like to acknowledge and thank Brian Johnston, who taught me everything I know about recreation planning, and without whose advice and support this book could not have been written. To Geoffrey Godbey, Tom Goodale, Dan Dustin, Jim Murphy, Gene Lamke, Mike Mahon, Ralph Nilson, and Dennis Hrycaiko, my sincere thanks.

I would like to acknowledge the many students who, for the past twenty-four years, patiently participated in my planning classes and from whom I learned as much as I taught. To my wife, Pat, for her advice and support and children Daniel and Jessica, who didn't always understand what I did, but liked having a "professor of fun" as their father.

Finally, I would like to thank the people who assisted me in writing this book, including editor Nat Cole, a talented wordsmith and the original DIY guy from Okeover Inlet; Tom Goodale for editorial input; Daniel Harper for his passionate photographic eye; and Colleen Plumton for assistance with editing and content. Every effort has been made to accurately reference the ideas and creative works of others. Please accept my apologies for any information contained herein that has not been accurately credited. If notified, corrections will be made in future editions.

Section I
Planning Principles and Process

1.0 Planning Defined

1.1 Introduction to Area and Facility Planning

This section provides an overview of area and facility planning related to the development of indoor and outdoor sport, recreation, and cultural facilities. There is also information about the relationship between planning and other management functions, definitions of various types of recreation planning, and the principles, strategies, and methods employed in the predesign planning process.

Most public recreation facilities in Canada were developed during a period of dynamic growth in recreation during the 1960s and early 1970s. Across the country, many communities built Centennial arenas or pools to commemorate Canada's 100th anniversary in 1967. In Winnipeg, for example, of the 24 indoor arenas owned and operated by the city, 14 were constructed during a ten-year period between 1967–1977, and 11 of 13 city-owned indoor pools were constructed during this time frame (PUFS Report, 2005).

Today, while new and improved facilities are needed to accommodate the changing requirements of consumers, the challenge for many recreation agencies is aging infrastructure that translates into expensive upgrading or replacement of obsolete facilities. This is particularly difficult for small communities with declining and aging populations that rely on taxes to build new facilities. While this book focuses on the process of new facility development, it also introduces strategies such as preventive maintenance management systems (PMMS), facility life cycle planning, and strategic and business planning, all-important elements in the development of sustainable facilities.

1.2 Area and Facility Planning Defined

The use of the term "area" may be confusing in the context of parks and recreation planning, but generally refers to space for something, and in this context it is considered to be synonymous with the more familiar term "open space." Danish urban designer Jan Gehl (in Urban Open Space, 2003) describes urban open space as "the life between buildings." In his landmark publication defining park standards, Wright (1976) defined open space as:

> "All land and water, both publicly and privately owned, that is open to the sky and reasonably accessible to freely chosen activity or visual exploration, and that serves people and nature in an educative, aesthetic, productive, protective, or recreative way."

While many people limit their definition of open space to active and passive designated parks, Wright's definition encompasses a broader and more comprehensive interpretation. This definition suggests that open space could include, but not be limited to, areas such as parks, boulevards, buffer strips, green belts, lagoons, retention ponds, utility rights of way, escarpments, and trails. These examples help define the components of the open space system, and each provides various benefits to the public and the community. A later section of this book describes in more detail the purpose, function, and organization of the open space system.

A facility is broadly described as a built environment to facilitate activity. For the purpose of this book, facility refers to both indoor and built structures designed or available to accommodate active and passive leisure and recreation programs and activities. As an example, facilities could include arenas, pools, theaters, community centers, curling rinks, soccer pitches, ball fields, wading pools, running tracks, golf courses, arboretums, fitness centers, and health clubs.

Planning is a systematic process leading to the achievement of desired objectives. In broader terms, it is seen as "a process by which a community or agency perceives the future, articulates its objectives, assesses its resources, and considers alternatives" (Balmer, 1988). In this context, planning can also be seen as a problem-solving process using relevant information and applying critical thinking to realistic options and alternatives.

John Friedman, in Retracking America (In Planning Recreation,1985, p. 9) defines planning in two ways: allocative and innovative. Allocative planning is a "basic form of planning concerned with the actions that affect the distribution of limited resources among competing users." Innovative planning is concerned with "actions that produce structural changes in the guidance system of society; it is essential to the continued structural growth of a social system and, consequently, to development."

In the public (local government) recreation subsystem, allocative planning presents the primary challenge for planners and managers. Deciding where and how to allocate limited resources, as demands and competition for resources increase, requires skillful planning. What communities require are strategies and techniques that increase objectivity and minimize special interest group pressures in setting priorities for resource allocation (see PERC Priority Rating System, Chapter 9.4).

It is equally important that public sector planners and managers practice innovative planning and are creative in their approach to problem solving, service provision, resource allocation, and facility development. In the absence of innovation and creativity, there is a risk that communities will fall into traditional patterns of development rather than be responsive to the changing needs and interests of the public they serve.

Planning (Figure 1.1) is based on knowing where you are today in terms of capacity and resources (Point A), where you want to be at some point in the future (Point B) in order to achieve the dreams and aspirations of your constituents, and assembling the resources necessary to achieve that goal.

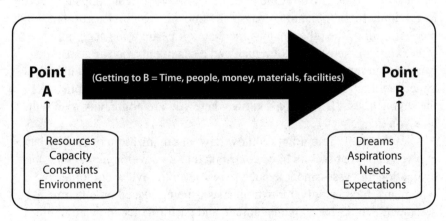

Figure 1.1 Planning Defined

1.3 Context for Planning and Management

Ted Storey, (in Planning Recreation, 1985, p. 8) believes that "planning is the process of deciding where you want to go and how you are going to get there; managing is the process of getting there; getting the right things done through the effective use of human, fiscal, and material resources."

When viewed in this context, Storey's observation suggests that planning is not an isolated activity, but rather one of the essential components of an integrated management process that involves five key functions: planning, organizing, staffing, directing, and controlling (evaluation).

Edgington (2001) defines management in operational terms as the organization of human, physical, and fiscal resources around specified goals to achieve efficiency and effectiveness. Efficiency is determined by the amount of those resources consumed as measured by the ratio of program costs versus revenue, facility capacity versus use, and performance by actual output versus established standards.

Effectiveness relates to the extent to which goals have been achieved. Measures of effectiveness involve an assessment of the quality of the service, the degree to which goals have been met, the external impact the service has had, and the internal impact on the health/resources of the organization or facility. Achieving efficiency and effectiveness are critical outcomes of planning and managing resources and facilities appropriately.

Unfortunately, both planning and evaluation have suffered in many organizations because these functions have not been seen to be as important as "doing." They are management functions that are left to consider when time allows. All too frequently they are ignored because there never seems to be enough time to do all of the important things that need to get done. In fact, planning may be the most important function in the process if all of the other management activities are to be accomplished effectively. In the absence of a plan and a statement of clear goals, there is a risk that management will occur in an ad hoc fashion without a clear understanding of what it is the organization is trying to accomplish. As the saying goes, "If you don't know where you are going, any road will take you there."

It is equally important to know how an organization or facility has evolved and what factors have contributed to its development. Outcome evaluation and assessment is one process used to review compliance with plans. Increasingly, more emphasis is being placed on outcome assessment, benefit-based management, and performance indicators as a component of the management process. This book will outline strategies necessary to undertake effective outcome assessment, particularly related to predesign planning or feasibility of new facility development.

Predesign facility planning is also frequently undervalued and seen by some as an unnecessary use of time and resources. In reality, facility planning and feasibility assessment are critical investments in the decision-making process that can result in significant savings in time and money. The facility planning process can help determine the cost and benefit of various development options and predict whether a facility will be cost-effective and financially sustainable over the long term. Before designing and building a facility, these are factors that every facility proponent should address.

1.4 Benefits of Planning and Evaluation

While attitudes toward planning and outcome assessment may differ, it is clear that any process designed to anticipate likely outcomes and the implications of decisions are worthwhile and an integral component of competent resource management. Simply put, planning can prevent bad decisions and costly errors.

The initial step in the planning process is to formulate appropriate goals and policies and to test them. Planning allows an agency to be proactive rather than reactive. The agency is able to anticipate the implications and impact (social, economic, and environmental) of decisions, rather than having to fix things after they have occurred. In this regard, planning helps an agency gain perspective on problems, develop realistic alternatives, and formulate a course of action that is more likely to succeed.

Planning is a useful tool to guide decision making and establish priorities for resource allocation using hard data and scientific information. This is particularly useful when resources are limited and choices need to be made between competing interests. Developing a well-researched, evidence-based plan can reduce the influence of special interest groups and ensure that decisions are made without undue bias. A plan is also beneficial in that it sets out the rationale and justification for resource allocation.

The planning process is of great benefit because it requires an agency to take stock of its current assets by undertaking a qualitative and quantitative inventory before new initiatives are considered. The asset inventory can then be used to develop appropriate service standards and supply guidelines or to test the current supply of facilities and services against accepted industry standards for service provision.

Given that the planning process is open and comprehensive, the real benefit is that it will engage consumers (members, participants, and the general public) in the process and lead to decisions based on the areas of greatest need. Consumer/public involvement is an important means to communicate, create awareness, and gain cooperation. If the consumer/public is involved in the process, there is a better chance they that will endorse the plan and support its implementation.

Evaluation is a critical step in determining if goals have been met, resources have been allocated appropriately, and positive change has occurred. Another benefit of evaluation and outcome assessment is that it allows an agency to modify and update plans as the environment changes, and to ensure compliance with goals over the long term.

1.5 General Planning Principles

The key goals of planning are to improve the quality of decision making, achieve greater efficiency and effectiveness, inject long-range considerations into short-term decisions, and ensure that the interests of the public (consumer, member, or user) are considered.

The community recreation system has three components. It comprises the public subsystem, the commercial subsystem, and the voluntary not-for-profit subsystem. While each of these sectors in the community recreation system is driven by different goals and motives, there are some generic planning principles that apply equally to each sector.

Common Planning Principles

1. Plans should reflect the mission, goals, objectives, and targets of the agency.

It is surprising, but not unusual, to find agencies and organizations today that don't have current goal statements or, more often, don't use the goals they have developed to guide decision making. If goals don't form the basis for planning and decision making, it is far too easy for an organization to lose its way and become engaged in activities and initiatives that have little to do with the reason the organization was originally developed. Section III of this book presents a comprehensive discussion of goal setting and why it is so important in the planning process.

2. Plans should be carried out in consultation with the people (consumers, members, users) affected by the plan.

Planning strategies require the involvement of the people who will have an impact on the implementation of the plan as well as people who will be affected by the plan. There are many challenges to undertaking this process in a way that will result in decisions that reflect the best interests of the agency and the people it serves. Care must be taken to ensure that bias is minimized and that the interests of the minority are respected. Section VII of this book deals with the issues of demand analysis, needs assessment, and the role of public participation in the process.

3. Planning must be comprehensive, inclusive, integrated, and responsive.

Reid (1998) stresses the importance of utilizing a comprehensive systems approach to recreation planning. His view is based on the premise that recreation planning can't be done in isolation and must be done as a set of activities that, when combined, provide a complete overview of the system being planned. As an example, this approach recognizes that planning a new recreation facility without considering the impact of program planning would be shortsighted. This principle emphasizes the need to look at the relationship between systems to ensure a plan is comprehensive and inclusive. The principle applies equally to the public, commercial, and not-for-profit sectors. It would be shortsighted to plan a commercial recreation facility without considering the supply of competing facilities and the impact that surrounding developments would have on the viability of the project.

4. Plans should be innovative, imaginative, dynamic, and flexible to accurately reflect the needs of a changing society.

Reid (1998) encourages planners and managers to ensure that the focus of planning is on innovation rather than growth and that the emphasis of planning be on needs from a social and psychological perspective rather than from a program perspective. Engaging consumers, users, and the public in this process is critical and suggests the process is as valuable as the outcome. In this regard, planning is seen as a means to an end, not an end in itself. It should be viewed as a process, not a product. The process has value beyond the creation of a report or a facility, particularly if it results in a better informed community, improved cooperation in decision making, and consumers and constituents who are fully engaged in working together to achieve goals.

5. Plans should be realistic and achievable.

It goes without saying that plans that are not realistic will not likely be achievable. Plans that are unduly influenced by special interest groups or poorly designed and executed are more likely to be unrealistic. To avoid this, it is essential that planners use facts and information to guide their decisions, not dreams and aspirations. It is equally important that bias be minimized in the process. A "field of dreams" approach may make great movie material but has no place in a well-designed planning process. It is irresponsible to approach facility development on the basis of "build it and they will come," particularly if public funds are used in the development of the project. The consequence of error is too great.

6. Plans must be reviewed regularly to ensure relevance.

Plans are based on a set of assumptions and predictions about likely future events and circumstances. The pace of change is accelerating at an alarming rate. Developing a facility from dream to reality can take five years on average.

Changes in the internal and external operating environment of an agency make long-range planning extremely difficult. It is, therefore, essential that continual monitoring of a plan be undertaken to ensure that assumptions and predictions made in the development of the plan remain accurate and relevant throughout the process. If the basis for recommendations in the plan is no longer relevant, then the plan must be changed to reflect the new reality.

1.6 Approaches to Planning

There are a number of schools of thought regarding the best approach to planning. While some experts emphasize past activities and participation as the best predictors of future program and facility needs, others believe economics (demand manipulated by cost) represents the best determinate of facility needs.

David Foote (1996), for example, believes that demographics are largely responsible for determining future trends and behavior, so that if you understand the impact of age, gender, and other demographic variables, you can accurately predict human behavior and, therefore, future facility use and consumption. Following are five common approaches to planning.

1. Resource Approach

The resource approach to recreation planning suggests that physical or natural resources determine the amounts of recreation opportunities. In this approach, the emphasis is on the resource rather than the user. This is one approach landscape architects use in the development of parks and open spaces. They examine environmental factors on a site such as soil and subsoil conditions, light, vegetation, wind exposure, and slope. These conditions often determine the best use of the site, the type of facilities the site can support, and the carrying capacity of the site.

The resource approach could also be associated with the "build it and they will come" approach where the focus is on developing resources and, once available, it is assumed that people will use them.

2. Activity Approach

The activity approach is based on the belief that past participation in selected activities is the best predictor of future program and facility use. This approach suggests that supply creates demand.

While this approach can be useful, it ignores the possibility of new trends and emerging activities that users are not familiar with and does not reflect the changing needs and interests of participants throughout the life cycle.

3. Economic Approach

The economic approach to recreation planning is based on the premise that economic resources determine the amount and type of activities people will consume. The economic approach could also be a factor in strategically locating certain types of facilities and services based on the economic status of residents in the surrounding area. In this regard, it is suggested that supply and demand are manipulated by price and cost/benefit analysis.

One economic theory of recreation participation is described as the elasticity of demand. This theory suggests that as the price of something goes up, the consumption or use of the product or service goes down, and that every service has its economic threshold where price can affect the viability of a facility or service.

4. Behavioral Approach

The behavioral approach is based on the premise that planning should recognize behavior, motivation, experience, satisfaction, and preferences as the best predictors of facility and program use. The antithesis of this approach would be to examine constraints or limitations that prevent people from participating. If constraints can be minimized, use and consumption of facilities and services should increase.

5. Combined Approach

Many factors affect the development and sustainability of programs and facilities. Used in isolation, each approach has limitations and provides a narrow view of the dynamic and changing needs of consumers. Therefore, it is unwise to rely exclusively on any one type of approach or data set to accurately predict the viability and feasibility of future developments. A combined approach to planning that looks broadly at all of the influences on future program and facility needs is likely to provide the most accurate prediction of what will work best.

Section II identifies various factors that must be considered when undertaking a program or predesign facility plan.

1.7 Planning Activities by Sector

The Community Recreation System involves the public (federal, provincial, and local/municipal), commercial (private), and voluntary/not-for-profit sectors. Although each sector is motivated by different goals and different service standards, the planning process is for the most part generic and can apply to each of the sectors equally.

Public Recreation Planning

The public sector includes all types of facilities, programs, and services that are tax-supported by local/municipal, provincial, and federal governments. The primary motive for the development of public facilities is to provide equitable access to recreation opportunities and serve people who, for many reasons, might not otherwise have an opportunity to participate. Public facilities are usually subsidized by tax support and operate on a "pay as you go" basis. The development of programs and facilities is justified on the basis of public good. A key requirement for public recreation facility planners is to engage citizens in the process and ensure a balanced approach, thereby meeting the broad range of needs for facility development given the resource limitations of tax-supported development.

Voluntary/Not-for-profit Planning

The voluntary sector is motivated by service to its clients and constituents. This sector includes thousands of communities of interest represented by clubs, associations, and charitable organizations. Communities of interest are formed to serve the unique needs of their clients, customers, and participants. In this sector there are sports-governing bodies, visual and performing arts groups, social service agencies, cultural organizations, clubs, and community centers.

Frequently, this sector receives public support for facility developments because they also provide services that meet public service objectives but can't be justified solely using tax support. The greater degree of compliance to public service objectives, the greater chance a not-for-profit project will have for support.

The operation of programs and facilities in this sector seeks to break even on operation and achieve long-term viability and sustainability. The not-for-profit sector relies heavily on volunteers to offset operating costs and achieve the goal of sustainability.

Commercial

The commercial (private) subsystem engages in facility development for the sole purpose of making a profit. Commercial developments typically rely completely on private investment to build the facility and charge fees that will cover all operating costs as well as provide a financial return to the owners and partners in the project.

Typically, commercial facilities try to avoid competition with public facilities that are heavily subsidized. The types of commercial recreation facilities that are frequently developed include theaters, bowling alleys, pool halls, marinas, theme parks, fitness centers and health clubs. In recent years, there have been some commercial (private) arenas developed where the market can support such initiatives. There have also been a few commercial pools developed, but typically they are built in conjunction with other types of development such as shopping malls or hotels that use recreation facilities to complement their main enterprise and increase their competitiveness in attracting customers.

Cooperative development of sport and recreation facilities between the public and commercial sector can occur if the project is seen to meet both public and private service objectives. This frequently occurs, for example, when major large-scale facilities are developed for national and international games or for professional sporting events.

P3s—Public/Private Partnerships

For many years, local governments have used various forms of cooperative development agreements to minimize reliance on tax dollars to provide and operate a variety of municipal services including recreation. These arrangements have varied from the complete privatization of municipal parks and facilities and services to more modest arrangements such as contracting out concessions, providing land for worthy community projects, and joint community-schools developments. A recent report on innovative sources of funding for infrastructure renewal (2006) sets out seven variations of partnerships from public owned and fully subsidized to privately owned and operated. Cooperative partnership arrangements can apply to any one of the community recreation subsystems, and the underlying objective is to ensure that each partner in the process shares the costs and benefits equally. This approach can result in the development of facilities that would not otherwise be possible and can minimize the impact on the general tax-paying public, placing more responsibility on the actual users of the facility.

In Winnipeg, for example, there are many examples of public/private partnerships with respect to the development of infrastructure, including the MTS Centre. Significant public taxpayer dollars were contributed to the project because of the long-term economic benefits to the city and province. In addition, the MTS Centre has an agreement with the City of Winnipeg that allows access to the facility for community groups and organizations.

A new approach to cooperative development is called P3s or public/private partnerships. In this approach, the private sector constructs the facility and leases it back to the municipality. Municipalities have used this approach to build bridges, roads, and recreation facilities for mutual benefit.

1.8 Types of Plans

1. Community (General) Plan—Plan Winnipeg

Winnipeg's general plan (2000) is called Plan Winnipeg 2020 Vision. It sets out the framework for development and provides the policy direction for all municipal services within the corporate boundaries of Winnipeg. The general plan deals with land use, transportation, subdivision planning, economics, environmental protection, public safety and parks, recreation, and social services. Essentially, the general plan established the standards for municipal development that define the quality of life in the community. All other plans to follow must be consistent with the principles, policies, and standards adopted in the general plan.

2. Parks and Recreation Master Plan

A parks and recreation master plan is a comprehensive, long-range planning document that sets out strategies for the orderly development of all services within the jurisdiction of the local government parks and recreation authority. The master plan includes plans for managing current recreation and parks resources and establishes the standards, rationale, resource requirements, and timeline for future parks and recreation program and facility requirements.

3. Facility Feasibility Study

A facility feasibility study generally provides the detail and justification for developing a new park or facility that might have been identified as a priority in the parks and recreation master plan. It is also a process that commercial developers go through when contemplating building a commercial recreation facility. The feasibility or predesign study is the first step in the facility development process that outlines in detail the benefits, impact, and costs associated with the development of the facility and specifies the standards, criteria, and rationale for its development.

In this regard, the study determines the most appropriate course of action from a number of alternatives and helps determine whether the new facility is both desirable and feasible in terms of its long-tern sustainability. The feasibility study also defines the "building program" or program of requirements for the facility based on the predicted use and uses of each space being considered. It also defines the size, shape, quality, and environmental conditions for each component of the building.

4. *Strategic Plan*

Strategic planning has become a popular approach to organizational growth and development. While there are many ways to define strategic planning and various development models, at the heart of the process is the "S.W.O.T." process (Strengths, Weaknesses, Opportunities, Threats). An organization is able to develop the strategies necessary to move forward successfully by minimizing weaknesses and threats while building on strengths and capitalizing on opportunities.

Perhaps the most succinct definition is one by Balmer (1988) who defines strategic planning as:

> "a process through which an organization envisions its future and develops the necessary procedures and operation to achieve that future. It is goal directed and issue based. It clarifies the business of an organization and responds to key current issues affecting the organization's ability to deliver and remain relevant."

5. *Business (Financial) Plan*

Business planning has become an essential tool to evaluate the viability and sustainability of organizations, programs, services, and facilities. For organizations and businesses seeking support for their initiative, a business plan is a required element. In the public sector, governments require a business plan before they will consider grants, partnerships, and co-development of initiatives. In the commercial sector, banks require a business plan in advance of providing loans and financing.

A business plan takes the strategic planning process one step further by outlining in detail the business the organization is in, the long-term target market and demand for the product or service, and the long-term financial viability of the initiative.

6. *Other*

There are other types of plans that agencies develop to examine specific needs, issues, or services, and the form they take will depend on the needs and circumstances of the community. These can include policy and systems plans, program development plans, marketing and communication plans, PATH planning (See Figure 7.4—PATH Process, p. 73), life cycle facility plans, and maintenance management plans.

Each of the above types of plans will be discussed in detail in sections to follow.

1.9 Keys to Successful Planning

A common question often asked of planners and consultants is whether their plans ever get implemented. Given that a plan reflects "a snapshot in time," it may not be surprising that the details or portions of the details of a plan may change before implementation. The more important question is whether the principles outlined in the plan form the basis for good decision making as time passes and the environment changes.

There is no substitute for planning in the overall resource management process. However, not every plan or planning process achieves what it is intended to do. When this occurs, it is usually the fault of a flawed planning design or process that for any number of reasons goes astray. Following are some of the factors that can affect the success of a plan and the likelihood of implementation.

1. Leadership

There are two essential ingredients to success. One is a well-designed plan, and the other is effective leadership capable of carrying out the plan. If either is lacking, then most plans will be doomed. There are too many cases where plans have been skillfully developed, but the people responsible for implementation of the plan are either not capable or not committed to the process.

2. Commitment

Plans can be threatening in that by their very nature they demand accountability, raise expectations, and set goals against which progress can be measured. Implementation takes leadership and initiative, and for too many managers, the status quo is a much more comfortable place to be.

If a plan is done well, it should involve all stakeholders and reflect consensus on the direction and focus of the organization or initiative. For some managers, consensus minimizes their ability to control the process and put their own stamp on the organization. When this occurs, the implementation of a plan will be affected.

3. Objectivity

If a plan is developed in an inclusive manner with the interests of all stakeholders in mind, then it should minimize the influence of special interest groups that can often hijack the process for their own benefit.

4. Creativity

Recognizing that each community, project, and situation is unique should lead to the development of creative and unique plans and solutions that stand a better chance of being implemented. Duplicating or borrowing something that might have worked well elsewhere and assuming that it will work in other situations will not produce creative community-specific solutions.

2.0 Planning Process

2.1 Introduction to the Planning Process

This section of the book outlines the steps involved in the process of planning and the type of information that is critical to the development of a plan. It also introduces the factors that affect planning and development decisions and emphasizes the importance of getting accurate information.

    While there are generic approaches to planning that would apply to the development of any type of a plan, each planning exercise is unique, and therefore the process must be tailored to fit the circumstances. For example, the process used to develop a strategic plan is considerably different from that used to complete a facility feasibility study. While all plans should include a statement of goals, the method by which goals are developed and monitored will vary from one plan to the next. In this regard, one size does not fit all.

2.2 Eight-Stage Approach to Planning

The following section outlines eight steps that could apply generally to any process involving planning for recreation programs, facilities, and services. While the illustration (Figure 2.1, p. 19) appears to represent a linear or step-by-step approach, it should be recognized that planning is circular, integrated, and continuous. This means that as information and data are collected and consultation occurs, the planning process must be flexible and evolve to reflect emerging information. For example, while public consultation is one step in the process, in reality it should occur throughout the process.

Each step will be described briefly below and in more detail in the sections to follow.

STEP 1. Goals for the Plan

The process used to develop a plan needs to be comprehensive in reviewing all contributing factors, inclusive of all partners in the process, dynamic and imaginative in approach, and circular rather than linear. The process designed to develop a plan should reflect these principles.

The first step involves setting goals for the plan and a careful consideration of what the planning process is intended to achieve. There should be consensus among the proponents of the plan that there is sufficient benefit and merit in developing a plan to warrant the time and expense involved.

Sample Goals: Facility Feasibility Study

Goal 1. To develop a comprehensive feasibility study that will confirm the need for a new arena in Communityville.

Goal 2. To ensure that the community is involved in the planning process.

Goal 3. To determine that there is sufficient demand for the use of a new arena, thereby ensuring its long-term sustainability with minimal reliance on public subsidy.

STEP 2. Terms of Reference

Once the goals for the plan are agreed upon and a decision has been reached to proceed, the next step should be to consider carefully why the plan is needed and how it will be used, how it will be developed, what information and factors the plan needs to include, when it should be completed, and by whom.

Developing a plan or undertaking a study can be done internally through a self-study process or externally using a planner, consultant, or facilitator. The choice of approach should be carefully considered, and a number of factors need to be weighed. Planning can be time-consuming, and unless this activity is part of the job description of an existing employee, it can divert his or her energy away from day-to-day responsibilities. Using the self-study approach might save money on consultants but costs equally as much in staff time. Planning also requires specialized expertise, and if this skill set is not available in the organization, it may have to be contracted externally. It may also be healthy for the organization to use an external third party to assist with a planning project to ensure objectivity and minimize bias in the study conclusions.

Whether it is decided to undertake the plan internally or externally, a study/planning committee should be appointed to oversee the process and make decisions on behalf of the organization. Terms of reference should be developed to guide the process, monitor progress, maintain focus, and consider in advance what is to be accomplished. If it is decided that external expertise is required, then terms of reference can form the basis of a request for proposals (RFP) and qualified planners and consultants invited to submit proposals on a competitive basis. If this is the case, an RFP (See Appendix A—Sample RFP) should request detailed information about the consultants, the study approach they will use, their experience to undertake the study, and the conditions under which they will carry out the work (time, costs, relationship with the study committee). The RFP should also contain information that explains to the consultants what the committee is looking for and how their proposal will be judged.

STEP 3. *Environmental Assessment*

This step involves the collection of data related to both the internal operating environment of the agency and the external environment affecting the operation of the agency.

Internal Environment relates to the capacity of the organization to accomplish its goals based on the human, physical, and financial resources it has available. The internal environmental data affecting a plan include:

a. Mission and goals of the agency: Is the plan/planning activity under consideration consistent with the purpose, mandate, and mission of the organization? It is essential that there be consistency between the mandate of an organization and the plans it is developing.

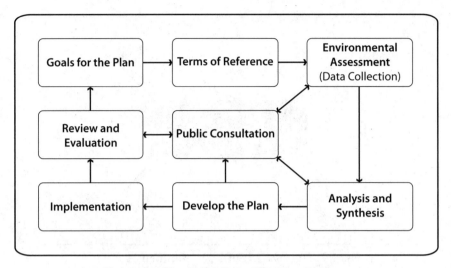

Figure 2.1 The Eight-Step Planning Process

b. Inventory: Taking stock of the current supply and capacity of the programs, services, and facilities of the agency is a critical step in understanding where there may be shortcomings, inadequacies, and unmet needs. Information about the quantity and quality of existing resources and how they can be and are being used is critical to the outcome of any plan.

c. Resources (budget, staff, volunteers): An analysis of the internal resources indicates what the capacity of the organization is or what additional resources might be needed to successfully implement the recommendations that will result from the plan. The type of information that is needed is a review of the past five years of budget and financial statements, staff profiles and skills, and volunteer support available.

d. Policies and Practices (standards): The policies and practices of an organization provide a sense of the culture of the organization and its capabilities to adapt to change. For example, policies that regulate facility use, user fees and public subsidy, joint-use or lease agreements, and cooperative facility development policies greatly assist future planning. There may also exist internal standards that guide development of new facilities (e.g., one indoor arena per 25,000 population) that need to be reviewed in the context of the planning activity.

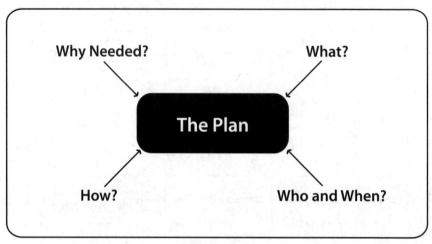

Figure 2.2 Terms of Reference

External Environment refers to local, national, and international events and circumstances from outside the organization that can have an affect on the organization over which there may be little or no control. The types of external influences affecting a plan include:

a. Needs and Preferences: A consumer/public needs assessment is an integral component of the planning process and is invaluable in determining the priorities and preferences of the potential users of a facility or service. Assessment can be carried out in a variety of ways, but again it is critical that the approach taken be specific to the community, organization, or facility for which the planning is being done.

b. Demand/Use/Consumption: Demand for a product, program, or facility can be measured by calculating current use, expressed demand through survey research, or comparative demand by examining use of similar programs or facilities elsewhere. Demand can be influenced by many factors such as cost, proximity to the service, knowledge about the service, and the skills needed to utilize the program or facility. It is important in undertaking a demand analysis to consider all of these factors and weigh their likely impact on use and consumption.

c. Demographic/Social Indicators (Community Profile): The characteristics and profile of users and potential users is a critical element in predicting the use and sustainability of a program or facility. Factors such as age, gender, ethnicity, income, and education all have an impact on participant skills, attitudes, motives, constraints, and behavior. Understanding the nature of leisure participation in a social and cultural context, as well as participation throughout the life cycle, are essential to accurate short- and long-term planning considerations.

d. Trends: In the context of recreation facility planning, a trend is a record of historical tendencies. Tracking the registration levels of youth soccer participants provides an historical record of participation. Trends are then used to make predictions about future events (participation) based on past experiences and assumptions about changes in the internal and external operating environment of the organization. While trends are one of the important factors in the planning process, it should be recognized that they are based on assumptions and predictions and, therefore, have limitations. The types of trends likely to impact future use of facilities and programs include changes in leisure participation and consumer behavior, demographic shifts, socioeconomic conditions, and new or innovative programs and facilities being developed.

e. Standards: There are various "industry" standards likely to impact on facility planning and development. Essentially, standards are norms that relate to internal policies or external regulatory conditions, and serve as guidelines for facility and program development. Standards may be of a qualitative or quantitative nature and affect the number, size, and conditions (safety/environment) of a facility. Standards are also useful comparative tools to judge the extent to which current facilities or proposed new developments vary from the norm or accepted industry standards.

The factors affecting program and facility development previously mentioned will be dealt with in more detail in the sections to follow. However, it is important to caution that these factors, if viewed in isolation, will provide a one-dimensional perspective. Therefore, it is important that they be viewed and analyzed collectively.

STEP 4. Consultation

This step requires that the planners and proponents of a plan consult in a meaningful way with the people (stakeholders) on whose behalf they are developing the plan, as well as with people who will be affected by the plan. The need for consultation applies equally to projects being developed in the public, commercial, and not-for-profit sectors. The ultimate goal of consultation is to engage end users in having a say in decisions affecting them and to attempt to make the plan better by expanding the sphere of input. There are many strategies and approaches to consultation that will be outlined in a section to follow, but again, the critical element is to ensure that the process is tailored to the plan or problem under consideration and that it be genuine and meaningful. If consultation is conducted effectively, the end result should be consensus among and between the stakeholders in the plan about the preferred course of action.

STEP 5. Analysis and Synthesis

Data analysis involves establishing criteria to weigh the various types of data that have been collected and establish the significance of each. In this process, the relationship between data sets (goals, demographics, supply, trends, demand, standards, public expectation) is also examined and subjected to a form of factor analysis.

Synthesis involves using the analysis of data to identify problems, suggest alternative solutions or actions, identify priorities, and weigh the impact of various alternatives and the consequences of the approaches/ decisions under consideration.

The ultimate goal of analysis and synthesis is to identify a preferred course of action and a set of priorities that form the basis of a plan.

STEP 6. The Plan

The final plan is usually presented in the form of a report that documents all of the data collected and alternatives considered. The plan is essentially a set of strategies designed to implement the preferred course of action leading to the achievement of the goals of the plan in the most efficient and effective manner. The plan outlines the rationale for the course of action chosen, the benefits and possible consequences of the plan, and identifies how the plan should be carried out, by whom, and over what time frame. The plan should also clearly identify the assumptions on which the preferred course of action is based so that actions and results can be monitored in light of the changing operating environment.

STEP 7. Implementation

Implementation is the phase of planning where the strategies, ideas, and actions recommended in the plan are carried out. It is during this phase that ideas become reality.

STEP 8. Evaluation and Review

Planning, if carried out appropriately, is not linear, but continuous and circular. It is important to remember that the objective of the planning process is to effect change, not simply to produce a report.

It must also be recognized that a plan is a set of predictions based on assumptions. Assumptions are based on the current operating environment and predictions about how it might change over time. For a plan to be relevant, it must constantly be reviewed to ensure that the predictions are accurate and the assumptions are valid. The time over which a plan remains valid and relevant will vary with the speed at which change occurs. At one time, long-range planning was considered to be five to ten years. The speed at which change occurs has accelerated, and it is advisable to constantly review plans and be prepared to revise strategies and priorities on an annual basis.

2.3 Planning Factors and Influences

An important part of the planning process is to examine factors that affect feasibility and desirability of a new recreation facility or program development. In examining issues of feasibility, both the internal organizational capacity and external community factors affecting consumption and use, viability, and long-term sustainability must be considered. A summary of some of these factors follows, and each will be reviewed in detail in subsequent sections of the book. Planning factors include:

1. Goals (objectives, policies, and practices)

The goals or purpose of a planning initiative should clearly indicate what the development of new or improved recreation facilities and programs are intended to achieve and how they contribute to the goals of the organization.

2. Supply Analysis

An inventory of existing resources (facilities, programs, staff, and financial capacity) should be compiled to evaluate the current service level and capacity to meet existing and future needs and demands.

3. Demographics and Community/Agency Profile

An assessment should be undertaken of the profile of the community. It should include information about the types of users, consumers, and clients you work with and how their age, gender, income, education, ethnicity, proximity to services, and past experiences are likely to affect use of recreation facilities, programs, and services.

4. Trends and Probable Futures

Changes in the internal and external operating environment occur over time, and they should be monitored to assess the impact they are likely to have on leisure behavior, facility demand, and use and attitudes toward leisure participation.

5. Demand Analysis

A measure of the gap between existing resources and public expectation will be a determining factor in the pressure to develop new and improved recreation facilities and services.

6. Public Consultation—Needs and Preferences

Communication with the public at all stages of the planning process is critical to understanding user needs and priorities, as well as achieving agreement on plans and strategies as they develop.

7. Standards—Qualitative and Quantitative

Industry standards regarding the supply of facilities and quality of development can be useful tools in determining appropriate measures to meet needs and demands for new and improved facilities.

Section II
Internal Organizational Planning Factors

3.0 Mission, Goals, Objectives, and Policies

3.1 Introduction to Goal Setting

The first step for any organization, or for a proposed facility, is to clearly articulate what it is you seek to achieve. In the absence of clear goals, organizations operate in an ad hoc fashion, unable to identify where they have come from or explain what they have achieved. In the recreation and leisure service system, there are a number of different types of goals that need to be identified, and they will vary with the type of organizations (public/commercial/not-for-profit) and the functions for which these organizations are responsible.

This section provides some examples, a process for defining values, goals and objectives, as well as ways to translate these statements into action plans to move the organization forward.

3.2 Hierarchy of Goal Setting

Goal setting can be a difficult and confusing exercise when you consider that the process involves a hierarchy that includes the definition and description of values and beliefs, operating principles, mission, goals, objectives, strategies, and action plans. Figure 3.1 illustrates the hierarchy of goal setting and the steps necessary to systematically develop statements that guide organizational development, decision making, and outcome assessment.

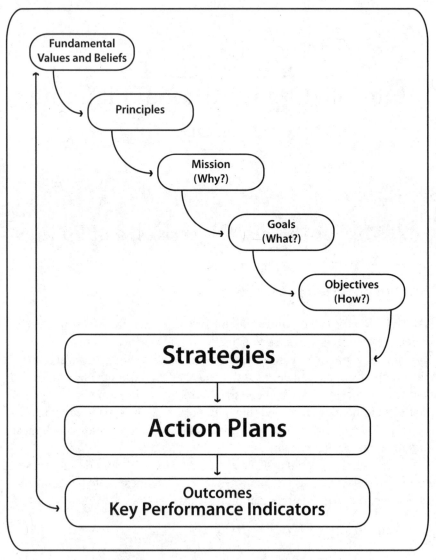

Figure 3.1 Goal Setting Hierarchy

3.3 Fundamental Beliefs, Values, and Principles

Before defining specific goals and objectives, organizations first need to examine the fundamental beliefs and values upon which their goals are based. For example, organizations involved in the delivery of recreation and leisure programs and services believe strongly that recreation contributes to individual and community growth, health, and development.

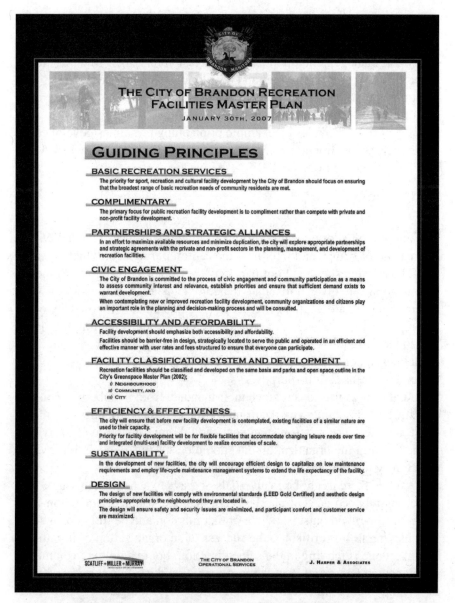

Figure 3.2 Guiding Principles (2007) City of Brandon

Public recreation organizations believe that recreation has equal importance to education and that people should not be denied access to recreation opportunities based on their ability to pay. As a result, communities support recreation and leisure through local taxation so that everyone can share in the benefits associated with recreation participation.

Values are guiding principles that reflect the fundamental beliefs of an organization upon which goals are based and are the preconditions governing management, operation, and decision making. Principles that relate to new facility initiatives and development should state clearly what the organization is prepared to support and the extent of its role and responsibility in undertaking any new development.

Figure 3.2 provides an example of planning principles developed to guide the City of Brandon when it developed its Recreation Facility Master Plan (Harper & Somers, 2007).

3.4 Mission

The mission of an organization usually defines its primary raison d'être or "reason for being" and interprets the central purpose for which it exists. The mission statement outlines why the organization exists. Some organizations are given a mandate to act by legislation or transfer of authority. For example, the Province of Manitoba mandates the City of Winnipeg to provide recreation for its citizens through enabling legislation in the form of the City of Winnipeg Act (2001). The act sets out the guidelines under which these services can be provided and allows the city to tax its citizens for this purpose.

Other organizations receive their mandate from members or constituents, who help define why the organization exists and identify its unique characteristics. The mission statement should represent a broad overview of the intent of the organization but should be specific enough to provide direction and articulate its unique attributes.

While there might be many goals or ways to achieve a mission, there can only be one central mission or mandate for an organization. Everyone involved must be aware of that mission and be fully engaged in achieving it. It is critical to the success of an organization or initiative that everyone is moving in the same direction. For example, the theme of the Canadian Parks and Recreation Association mission statement (2006) is "Healthy People in Healthy Communities," and it organizes its resources around goals designed to achieve that end.

3.5 Goals

Goals are statements that outline WHAT the organization will do to achieve its mission. They are still broad statements of intent, but specify the key areas or functions within the organization and outline how they contribute to its overall mission.

Goals should be developed for each key area of operation or responsibility to ensure they are comprehensive and inclusive. For example, if a plan is being developed for the construction of a new facility, the goals should address public consultation and user needs, quality of construction, financing, scope and scale of the facility, timelines, and critical path. Once the facility is complete, there should be goal statements that address some or all of the areas of responsibility such as management, operation, marketing, customer service, and maintenance. Goals are often categorized in the following way.

Governance and Management Goals

Governance goals describe how the organization manages itself. They often outline the operating principles or philosophy of the organization or describe the role and function of the organization in the broader community. They should also describe the decision-making process within the organization and compliance with the policies and guidelines governing the organization. These goals might include statements about quality, excellence, openness, transparency, and willingness to communicate with members and constituents.

Resource Goals

Resource goals refer to the management and allocation of human, physical, and fiscal resources entrusted to the organization. These goals might describe personnel practices, facility development guidelines, maintenance standards, and financial accountability measures.

Example: To manage the resources of the organization both efficiently and effectively, thereby guaranteeing the long-term viability of the organization and ensuring compliance with accepted industry accountability standards and practices.

Service Goals

Service goals might be considered output goals because they describe the development and production of services the organization seeks to deliver. These goals could include the organization's approach to program and facility development, strategies for communication with members, and commitment to partnerships and cooperative development.

Example: To develop recreation programs that meet the broadest range of public needs and ensure that they are affordable and accessible.

Goal 1. Historic Restoration, Preservation, and Maintenance

To restore the theatre to its original design, maintain it at the highest possible standards, and preserve it for the use and enjoyment of present and future generations.

Objectives:

1.1 Theatre Restoration

To carefully and accurately restore both the interior and the exterior of the theatre to its original condition utilizing accepted industry restoration conventions, standards, and practices.

1.2 Capital Development Plan

To develop a long-term capital improvement plan to restore the theatre to its original condition, establish priorities for development, and target sources of financial support.

1.3 Theatre Preservation

To develop a proactive long-term life cycle maintenance program designed to extend the life of the facility and minimize maintenance costs.

1.4 Ongoing Maintenance

To develop a high-quality, ongoing maintenance management system as a means to ensure cleanliness, safety, and a high level of customer satisfaction.

Figure 3.3 Sample Goals and Objectives—The Burton Cummings Theatre for the Performing Arts (2004)

Goal 1. Historic Restoration, Preservation, and Maintenance

To restore the theatre to its original design, maintain it at the highest possible standards, and preserve it for the use and enjoyment of present and future generations

Objective 1— Theatre Restoration: To carefully and accurately restore both the interior and the exterior of the theatre to its original condition utilizing accepted industry restoration conventions, standards, and practices.

Strategies	Targets and New Initiatives	Priorities and Timelines
1. Complete commemorative integrity statement required for federal funding program.	• Participate in interagency consultation process to develop statement.	Immediate: by June 30, 2003
2. Undertake review of 1992 Conservation Report and develop a comprehensive facility master.	• Plan to include architectual design, feasibility, environmental impact assessment, business plan, and economic impact assessment.	Immediate: Submit request for funding support to Centre Venture and Western Economic Diversification
3. Establish priorities for restoration and redevelopment projects.	• Restoration of lobby, reseating and carpeting, staging, men's smoking lounge, heating/cooling system, lobby addition, add elevator, restore marquee, entrance, and signage.	Long-term: Completed by February 2007
4. Apply for Community Places Grant to restore marquee, complete restoration of smoking room for temporary hall of fame, and install new signage.	• Phase One of Music Hall Development involved creating temporary home for hall in men's smoking room. • Complete feasibility study. • Execute capital campaign.	May 2003
5. Establish a reserve fund (for the restoration fee charged on all tickets) to provide matching funds for government grant projects.	• The proceeds from the restoration fee would provide approximately $40,000 in matching capital and restoration projects.	Immediate and ongoing

Figure 3.4 Sample Action Plan—The Burton Cummings Theatre for the Performing Arts (2004)

Outcome Goals

Outcome goals describe what the organization seeks to achieve by the provision of services and anticipated outcome of the service. They should be expressed in terms of benefits to the organization or to the participants and service users.

Example: To ensure that all employees and volunteers of our organization focus on providing the highest quality of customer service.

3.6 Objectives

Objectives are specific statements that indicate how an organization will carry out stated goals. It is generally acknowledged that objectives should be realistic and achievable, time specific and measurable (outcome/benefit based) statements.

Example (Harper & Doyle, 2004):

> Objective 1. "To increase the participation of youth (13–18 years of age) in fitness programs offered in our health club by 15% over the next 12 months."

3.7 Action Plan

The next step in the hierarchy is to outline strategies and actions necessary to achieve the stated mission, goals, and objectives. In recent years, more attention has been paid to outcome assessment or measurement, and most plans now include a statement of key performance indicators (KPI) or performance measures.

Once these have been agreed upon, it is much easier to measure how much actual progress has been made toward achieving goals and targets and then revise them to reflect the changing reality of the organization or service.

3.8 Guide to Writing Goals

The task of writing goals when none exist is extremely difficult, particularly when an organization has multiple responsibilities. Getting agreement and arriving at consensus is equally difficult when many people are involved in the process, often with different perspectives on issues, priorities, and direction.

There is no easy solution to this dilemma, but it is critical that all of the stakeholders and partners involved in the organization participate equally in the process. Unanimous agreement is unlikely, but there should be consensus on each of the major goals that are developed. Having achieved consensus will make management much easier and successful implementation more likely.

4.0 Supply Analysis

4.1 Introduction

Supply analysis refers to a comprehensive inventory of programs, facilities, and services described in both quantitative and qualitative terms. A meaningful inventory supplies all pertinent information about design, location, goals, costs, target market, size, and capacity of facilities and programs. This information provides a comprehensive profile of the factors that should be considered when either a reduction or increase in programs and facilities is contemplated. Once completed, the inventory can be compared to industry service standards and used to identify service gaps and facility deficiencies.

When developing a parks and recreation master plan or facility feasibility study in the public sector, it is important to know what private, commercial, and not-for-profit services are available so that they can be considered in the context of an overall plan and minimize unnecessary competition and duplication. It is equally important for a commercial facility planner to know where public and not-for-profit facilities already exist, so that a new facility can be strategically located to maximize potential use and profitability.

The purpose of an inventory is to accurately access existing services to determine if there is an oversupply or deficiency that needs to be corrected. The relationship between the human, physical, and fiscal resources of an organization requires that for inventories to be inclusive and comprehensive, each of these areas must be assessed.

This section provides guidelines for developing comprehensive program and facility inventories and discusses the relevance and impact of this information on planning and decision making.

4.2 Financial Capacity and Human Resources

The financial and human resources available to carry out the objectives of an organization, or to cope with change as it evolves, are critical factors to success. Every organization should have a human resource plan

Community	Program Category			
	Art	Generic/Social	Physical	Total
West Central	12/143	22/903	7/2532	121/3578
Northwest	29/329	66/3840	109/6080	204/10516
East Central	24/293	43/1713	65/5365	132/7371
North	5/53	59/1185	813951	145/5190
South	45/767	39/1163	101/4431	185/6361
Total	**115/1585**	**229/8805**	**443/22359**	**787/32749**
%	**14.6%**	**29.2%**	**56.2%**	

**Table 4.1 Summary of Program Supply by Category and Location
(Number of Programs / Participants)**

that includes an inventory and assessment of the skill set currently available. This information will be valuable in determining the impact new programs, facilities, and services will have on the current workforce and what training or hiring might be needed to compensate for the changing workforce requirements.

The financial capacity of the organization would be reflected in its business plan (see Chapter 13), and the impact of future program and facility changes would need to be incorporated into long-range financial projections to determine their feasibility and desirability.

4.3 Program Inventory

A comprehensive program inventory should include information about the program type, user profile, location, time of day, intensity, and frequency (number of hours/number of days) of participation, number of sessions, cost, and program capacity. A checklist for each program is a

Zone	Under 5	5-12	13-19	20-55	55+	Family	Total
West Central	13/228	53/1338	11/170	35/750	1/7	8/1025	121/3578
Northwest	25/1841	64/4690	24/1081	85/1944	1/5	7/1081	204/10516
East Central	46/1330	28/4312	10/126	37/924	1/6	10/673	132/7371
North	16/705	50/2578	11/253	60/1403	2/32	6/219	145/5190
South	14/535	61/334	20/425	71/1461	0/0	19/606	185/6361
Total	**114/4639**	**254/13250**	**76/1992**	**288/6482**	**5/50**	**50/3604**	**787/32749**
%	**14.5%**	**32.3%**	**9.6%**	**36.6%**	**0.12%**	**6.4%**	

Table 4.2 Summary of Program Supply by Age and Location

useful tool to collect information in a consistent manner and aid in analysis and comparisons over time.

Program type refers to major categories of activity such as sport, fitness, cultural programs, visual arts, performing arts, and social recreation. Collecting this information by program name will allow for analysis by classification.

Information about users and participants should include the age, gender, required skill level (beginner/advanced), and any other pertinent demographic and user profile data participants are willing to share. For example, if postal code information can be collected from the participants, service radius and program reach provides useful information for marketing programs.

The capacity of a program can be measured by the number of participants legally or comfortably accommodated by the program. Health and safety regulations, as well as program quality issues, regulate restrictions on participant limits. Calculating the defined capacity of a program is critical to understanding how well it will serve its intended market and meet its designed goals and targets.

Information about the time of day, location, and cost of the program is helpful when examining barriers and constraints to participation and establishing the best site and price for the service.

Once this information is collected, it can be used to analyze program availability and quality and to determine the extent to which the needs and demands of the users are being met. This information also indicates who is and who is not using the service and how gaps in service can be improved.

Table 4.1 is an example of one level of program analysis that illustrates the distribution of programs by category and location. This analysis is useful in determining whether all communities in the city are being served equitably. To better understand the issue of distribution, actual population levels in each community need to be considered. This table also illustrates that the preponderance of available programs are of a physical recreation nature.

Table 4.2 illustrates an analysis of program supply by age and community. While more information is needed about population distribution by community before a conclusion can be drawn, this analysis does provide useful information about service levels to various age categories. For example, if 20% of the population is over 55 years of age and less than 1% of the available programs are for seniors, it is very likely that this age group is underserved.

4.4 Facility Inventory

A facility inventory is not unlike the program inventory outlined and may be carried out using a predesigned checklist (see Appendix B, p. 177) that contains all of the pertinent information needed to analyze the supply (quantitative) and suitability (qualitative) of facilities that exist.

Designing a customized checklist for stand-alone or multiple facilities will assist greatly in developing consistent and reliable information. Maintaining and updating inventories on a regular basis will keep them current and relevant. A customized checklist also ensures that the data is collected consistently should more than one person be involved in the process.

The accuracy of information collected in the inventory is critical to facility planners and users alike. The planners rely on accurate information to calculate the capacity and potential for use of a facility. There are space standards governing organized sport. If facilities are used for competitive sport, it is important to ensure that fields, courts, gyms, ice surfaces, and pools are measured accurately to determine if they comply with the standards. There are many justifiable reasons that community facilities might not comply with the standards set for competitive or high-performance sport, and this should be reflected in the inventory.

Completing an accurate and reliable inventory is one of the steps in the planning process that provides information about "where we are today" with respect to the quality and quantity of facilities and programs. While there are many helpful resources available that can assist in developing your own facility checklist, it is important that the following factors be included.

1. Physical Description—Dimensions, Features, and Equipment

A detailed description of the site, facility, or space might be accompanied by a map or diagram of the site, including all components and features found there. When there are multiple facilities on one site or a multipurpose space, the inventory must highlight this. For example, if an inventory lists two softball diamonds and one soccer pitch that overlap, it is important to identify the primary use of the site, or the inventory will misrepresent the actual number of usable spaces. It is also important to know what ancillary and support facilities are available, such as parking, water stations, washrooms, concessions, and service buildings. This information helps a planner understand how the site functions (see Table 14.2, Open Space Components, p. 130).

Figure 4.1 Good Neighbours Senior Centre Membership by Postal Code

2. Current Use, Users, and Uses of Facility

The activities that a facility accommodates are critical to understanding how it functions. Not all activities that occur in a facility reflect the primary purpose for which it was designed. For example, while a squash court was designed for racquet sports, it can also be used for yoga, fencing, and two-on-two volleyball. Diversified use of space dedicated for a specific activity might represent a compromise in the use of space, or it might represent unmet facility requirements in the current inventory.

3. Long-Term Potential For Use

Inventories should include information about the flexibility, adaptability, and suitability of a space or facility to accommodate changing consumer needs and interests over time. Because of the high costs of facility development, components that can serve a variety of different needs contribute to the long-term viability and sustainability of the facility.

4. Service Radius/Reach

Recreation participation and facility use can be affected by many things. Among them is the location and proximity of the facility to the primary target market. While several factors affect choice and use of facilities, consumer proximity is a determining factor in the frequency and intensity of use. Postal code tracking is a means to visually represent "reach" or service radius of the primary users or members of a facility. Figure 4.1 (Harper, 2004) is an example of a service radius analysis using member postal codes of the Good Neighbours Senior Centre.

5. Qualitative Analysis

Inventories should be both quantitative and qualitative. A field or court might be the right size to accommodate the activity for which it is designed, but the quality of the space may limit the potential level of play or participation. A regulation-size soccer pitch with poor quality turf could limit its use for adult or high performance competition. A quantitative inventory might indicate a sufficient number of fields to accommodate all soccer groups in the community, but the quality of the fields might restrict the level of participation, creating demand for fields of a more suitable nature.

6. Classification—Level of Play

An assessment of the level of play (beginner, youth, adult, high performance) the field or facility is designed to accommodate should be included in the inventory. This is related to the quality of the space discussed above, but it also is affected by the design, layout, and site amenities. Chapter 14 provides a complete description of the systematic classification of facilities and open space and standards that apply to various levels of play.

7. Condition Assessment (Life-Cycle/Life Expectancy)

An inventory should include some indication of the current condition and life expectancy of the facility and its components. This information allows for long-term capital budget preparation and scheduled major maintenance and (life-cycle) replacement planning.

8. Potential for Expansion

Identifying information about the potential for expansion as needs change can greatly assist in long-range planning. It is also useful in the consolidation of multiple facilities on one site that can lead to greater efficiency, economies of scale, and efficient land use in future facility development.

9. Capacity

The capacity of a facility is defined by the number of users that can comfortably and effectively be accommodated in a given space. In this regard, each facility type and component will provide different levels of capacity based on the space available and the type and level of activity. The relationship between available capacity and current use is a critical factor in predicting when there is sufficient demand to warrant new or expanded facilities.

One of the facility planning principles discussed in an earlier chapter suggests that new facilities should be delayed when unused capacity exists. While this is not the only factor to consider, it represents an important consideration in long-term planning and decision making.

The efficient use of space is a related issue to capacity. If two people are using a space designed for fifty, the per-person cost to maintain the space will be difficult to justify and sustain. Information about the efficient use of resources and the capacity for use provides a picture of how effective a facility is in meeting its goals and targets.

The process used to define capacity and efficiency measures can be a complex task. The following section provides some models and examples to consider.

4.5 Defining Capacity and Efficiency Measures

— 4.5.1 Introduction

Many factors affect the degree to which a space or facility can accommodate its intended use. Some factors can be controlled while others cannot. The eventual number of participants that can be accommodated in a particular space varies according to the size, shape, and configuration of the space and the desired quality of the experience. Some measures of capacity are established by health and safety regulations, while others are established by participation standards, the nature of the activity, and the comfort of the participants.

As an example, safety regulations limit the number of patrons that can be in a theater or day-care center based on factors such as time required to safely exit in emergencies, air quality, staff/participant ratio, and patron comfort. The rules of the game establish the number of people that can be accommodated on a tennis court, soccer pitch, or ice arena for competition. The comfort and safety of participants limit the number of people that can be accommodated in a pool during public swimming, a fitness studio during an aerobics or yoga program, and an ice surface for hockey practice or figure skating training.

When contemplating the expansion of facilities, it is important to know how well and to what capacity present facilities are being utilized. Examining management, marketing, or program strategies is a cost-effective means to maximize use before adding costly new facilities that could go underutilized. While several factors need to be considered, use versus capacity is an important factor to accurately predict when downsizing or an expansion is warranted.

— 4.5.2 Evaluation, Assessment, and Efficiency Measurement

Facility planners and managers need to monitor and evaluate the status of their facilities on an ongoing basis to ensure they continue to operate in an efficient and effective manner. Facility assessment utilizes systematically collected data to monitor and judge the use and suitability of leisure facilities. Data collected through this process provide a benchmark from which to calculate present use versus predicted future demand and then design strategies to effect the changes necessary to ensure the effective and efficient use of all facilities.

Essentially, the process requires that measures be designed to assess the efficiency and effectiveness of the facility in meeting specific performance goals and targets.

Effectiveness

The effectiveness of a facility is a measure of the degree to which it achieves its defined goals and targets. Facility managers develop annual programs, financial and performance targets, and evaluate progress on an ongoing basis.

There may be many reasons a facility continually fails to meet its targets. It could be the result of poor programming, marketing, location, design, maintenance, or image. It could also be that the facility is obsolete and nearing the end of its life cycle. If this is the case, remedial action is needed.

Efficiency

Efficiency refers to the amount of human, physical, and fiscal resources consumed in the achievement of facility goals and targets. The objective of most organizations is to use the least amount of resources necessary to achieve goals. This practice results in the efficient operation of the facility or service. Efficiency can be measured in a number of ways, and managers need either to develop or adapt theoretical efficiency measures to meet their situation.

Three Measures of Efficiency

Following are three measures used to calculate the efficiency of a facility operation that are based on the targets set or standards developed for the operation.

1. Operating Efficiency

The operating efficiency of a facility can be measured by calculating the net revenue received from the operation or the number of staff hours required to operate the facility on an annual basis. These formulae provide a ratio of output versus input.

A. Cost Efficiency = Facility Expenses vs. Facility Revenues
B. Staff Efficiency = Service Hours vs. Staff Hours

In measuring cost and staff efficiency, it is important to relate the actual performance outcome to the goals for the facility. Private clubs have a profit motive and would not be satisfied with a deficit on operations that failed to deliver a dividend to shareholders. The goal of service clubs is to break even on their operation because they have no way to backstop losses that might occur.

The public sector, on the other hand, establishes a recovery threshold to achieve on operation. This is a political decision based on the extent to which public facilities should be paid for by users versus the

Type of Use/User	# of Uses Per Week	Hours of Use Per Week	Capacity Per Use	Total Capacity Per Week
Swim Club	12	12	30	360
Early Bird	7	15	150	1050
Parent Tot	3	5	60	180
Senior Social	3	5.5	200	600
Public Swim	8	13.5	300	2400
Swim Rentals	2	2	200	400
Adult Swim	5	8	200	1000
Family Swim	3	5.5	300	900
Aquasizes	4	6	70	280
Lessons	30	24.5	40	1200
Noon Swim	6	9	200	1200
Master Swim	1	1.5	100	100
Teen Swim	1	1.5	200	200
Fitness Club	7	8.5	70	490
Prenatal Fitness	1	1	70	50
Circuit	7	18.5	30	210
Adult Lessons	2	3	30	60
Private Lessons	2	3	40	80
Total	72	143		10,760

Table 4.3 Pool Capacity Per Week (In Swims)
(Note: The pool was open for 109 hours per week, but 143 hours of use was recorded due to multiple uses of pool at peak time)

general taxpayer. Due to the high cost of operating arenas and pools, many communities set recovery targets in the 40–60% range for these types of facilities and set their user fees accordingly.

The targets set for cost and staff efficiency provide a concrete basis from which to measure the efficiency of the facility operation and can be used to identify variables that need to be adjusted should the operation fall short of expectation.

2. Performance Efficiency Ratios (Actual Output vs. Standard Output)

Performance efficiency is a measure of the actual performance of a facility or its components versus industry standards and practices. This form of evaluation could allow managers to compare the performance of one arena against the average performance of several similar facilities to determine how efficiently it was operating relative to the others. It could also be done by comparing a given arena operation to standard operating expectations established by experienced arena operators.

This form of efficiency assessment has become known as benchmarking or best practices. Realistic benchmark indicators or targets are established as an operational goal and the performance of the facility and its components are measured against the benchmark. Best practices, on the other hand, are a means to assess facility performance against what are regarded as optimal operating targets and conditions to see if a particular facility measures up.

These assessment strategies provide useful tools to refine management practices to achieve greater efficiency in operations. They can also assist in determining when a facility may be obsolete or in need of a major overhaul.

3. Capacity/Utilization Efficiency

The method used to calculate a facility efficiency ratio involves dividing the attendance or use of the facility by its capacity to accommodate use.

$$\text{Facility Utilization Efficiency Ratio} = \frac{\text{Current Use}}{\text{Capacity of Facility}}$$

This method of assessment requires that accurate records be maintained and appropriate definitions of capacity be calculated if the information is to be useful.

Defining Use

Attendance, use, and participation numbers are easily maintained in facilities and for programs that require rigorous control and record keeping, such as pools, arenas, and fitness programs. This makes it possible to track the number of users in a particular space with a high degree of accuracy. Drop-in facilities, parks, play areas, trails, and outdoor courts are not generally monitored, and records of use and participation are more difficult to generate. Reliable and accurate user data and participation information is important information to consider when facility decisions are contemplated.

The actual number of users that can be accommodated in a facility will vary depending on the type and nature of the activity and the design and configuration of the space.

Defining Capacity

The real challenge is to accurately define the capacity of a facility or activity space so that meaningful measures can be made. The capacity of every facility type and activity space needs to be calculated based on different principles and operating assumptions. Capacity can be measured in terms of available space (area per person), hours of operation, or the design and amenities.

For example, pool use could be measured on the basis of square foot per person of space while the capacity of a golf course is based on the number of rounds or groups of four players that can safely and comfortably tee off during the hours of light available each day.

In addition, the program type and level of use varies considerably within the activity space. The number of people that can use a pool enclosure is based on a measure of swims per activity type. The capacity of swimming lessons is different than the number that can be accommodated during aquacizes. A one-hour hockey practice accommodates approximately 25 participants while one hour of public skating can accommodate 150 users.

Table 4.3 (see p. 44) lists various uses of a pool enclosure and the number of hours it is available for this purpose during the week. The capacity for use in each scheduled time spot differs due to the space required for the activity, the intensity of the activity and the level of supervision required. Once the capacity for each type of use has been determined, the actual number of participants is measured against the capacity to determine if the space is being used efficiently.

Following are four theoretical means to define capacity and each can be tailored or modified to fit the facility type and program use intended in the space.

1. Carrying Capacity

Carrying capacity is defined as the capability of natural resources to accommodate use without diminishing the quality of the activity or the resource. Carrying capacity can be established by undertaking an environmental impact assessment. To avoid deterioration of either the resource or the experience, resource management policies should be established and standards of use set.

The types of recreation facilities that are affected by carrying capacity are trails, fields, pitches, and diamonds that occur in natural areas and spaces. Management practices used to protect the resource include trail closing, limited hours of use per field/per week, temporary field closings during inclement weather, or retirement for extended periods to allow the field to recover.

2. Legal Capacity

Legal capacity refers to health, safety, and fire controls established by provincial legislation and municipal by-laws limiting the number of patrons that can occupy facilities and public gatherings. Most public facilities require operating licenses that designate the number of people who can occupy a particular space at one time. This includes theaters, restaurants, day-care centers, and pools, to name a few.

As an example, the number of patrons allowed in a pool enclosure at one time is regulated by the Manitoba Government Health and Safety Regulation 132/9. The regulation requires 1.5 square meters of water surface per person. The legal capacity of a standard pool tank of 325 square meters/1.5=216 patrons.

While this represents the legal capacity of the pool, the number of actual users varies with the activity in the pool. Using the legal capacity as the measure of efficiency would be extremely misleading, given that it is impractical to expect that when the pool is open there should always be 216 patrons using the space.

It is also unlikely that 216 patrons in the pool at the same time would provide a very high quality experience, and pool operators actually limit use at any one time to no more than 125–150 people in a standard 25-meter pool.

3. Optimal Theoretical Capacity

The optimal theoretical capacity of a facility would be 8,760 hours based on availability 24 hours each day, seven days per week, and 52 weeks of the year. The number of uses it could accommodate would be a total of the optimum use at any one time multiplied by the number of potential hours of use. This would mean that if a pool could accommodate 15 uses per day and public swim can accommodate 216 patrons per use (based on legal capacity), the total user capacity would be 1,182,600.

While this might represent the theoretical capacity, it in no way represents a realistic assessment of the capacity of a facility and can be misleading with respect to user needs and demands.

Factors that must be taken into consideration when calculating the capacity of a facility include climate, technology, facility design, program design, location, available space and configuration, management policies, and maintenance practices.

Facilities need down time for regular maintenance, lighting can increase the available capacity on fields, technology allows hockey to be played twelve months of the year in warm climate communities, and the cost and availability of staff can limit the hours of operation.

4. Functional Capacity

Facility planners need to develop a functional definition of capacity so that sound decisions can be based on realistic measures of use and capacity. The objective of the exercise is to determine when demand exceeds capacity or when declining use might indicate a reduction in service is warranted.

The functional capacity of each facility type needs to be defined individually because they each have different characteristics, variables, and constraints. For example, golf courses could calculate capacity on the basis of the number of foursomes that can comfortably play during the hours of available light between the predicted opening and closing date of the facility. Many golf course managers, however, use past experience as the best measure and calculate the average number of rounds played over the past five years as a benchmark of their capacity.

The challenge for facility managers is to establish a realistic measure of capacity and evaluate user levels so that appropriate decisions regarding expanding or downsizing facilities can be made.

Section III
External Planning Factors
and Conditions

5.0 Future Trends & Forecasting

5.1 Introduction to Trends and Probable Futures

The pace of change is accelerating as technology, globalization, and other related factors attempt to keep up with increased consumer demands. Consider the following events, and it is easy to see how the world around us is changing:

1. All telephone calls made around the world in 1984 and the equivalent of all e-mails sent around the world in 1989 now happen in one day.
2. When tele-messaging on mobile phones started about five years ago, there were 20 million messages sent every month. Today, 4 billion are sent every month.
3. The equivalent of all the science conducted in 1960 happens in one day today.
4. All of the foreign exchange dealings around the world in 1979 now happen in one day.
5. A year's worth of growth in the U.S. economy in 1830 happens in a single day today.
6. All of the world trade in the whole of 1949 happens in a single day today.

(Source: Journey Forward, 2003, The United Way, Winnipeg, Manitoba)

The reality of change makes it more and more difficult to predict the future with much accuracy or anticipate what impact change will have on society. It is nonetheless important to make an effort to try to anticipate the future and understand what actions are necessary today to prepare adequately for a likely scenario in the future. The process of planning essentially requires an ability to understand where we are today, predict what impact future events will have, prepare appropriately for change, and adjust accordingly to reality as it unfolds.

Godbey (2006) stresses the importance for leisure service practitioners to monitor change and understand the future. His view is that the "reinvention of leisure" is going on right now, and if we fail to pay attention, it will pass us by and render us irrelevant.

It is, therefore, important for leisure service practitioners and planners to understand the forces that create change and develop techniques to improve the accuracy of forecasts and the ability to predict change. When planning multimillion dollar recreation facilities, the consequences of error can be dramatic. The long-term feasibility and sustainability of facilities rely on accurate predictions and measures of demand and use. If they are in error, the facility will fail.

5.2 Defining the Conditions of Change

Events and circumstances that affect our way of life can occur gradually over time, or they may be very sudden. When change occurs gradually, we may not even be aware that things have changed because we learn to adapt as change occurs. This is called incremental or evolutionary change, and we may only be aware of this type of change if we reflect back over time and recognize what is different. Issues like global warming or gradual climate change over time would be examples of incremental change.

Another form of change is pendulum change, where events swing back and forth between two extremes. Changes in the popularity of political parties would be one example of pendulum change, and trends or fads in leisure participation and clothing fashions might be another. Over time, the popularity and participation rates in activities such as tennis, golf, and fitness can increase or decrease for a variety of reasons and are influenced by many factors.

When change occurs suddenly or without warning, it can have either a positive or a devastating impact, and we may have difficulty adapting in the short term. When a revolutionary new idea or way of doing things is presented, it can take time to adjust to this change. Revolutionary ideas or sudden events are described as a paradigm shift, where the way we view the world may change, and it is unlikely that we will return to our former views and behavior. This could happen when a natural disaster strikes and our living environment is impacted immediately, or if we experience a sudden illness that affects our way of life, forcing us to adapt to a new set of circumstances. Events that shake our confidence, sense of security, or trust can have this effect as well.

Understanding and anticipating the nature and pace of change is central to an ability to plan appropriately for the future.

5.3 Guidelines for Forecasting

No one can say with certainty what the future holds because there are so many interrelated factors and variables that affect change. There are, however, some techniques and strategies that can improve the accuracy of predictions. The accuracy of a forecast or prediction of future events relies heavily on the objectivity of the analyst as well as the source, quality, and reliability of the data used to make predictions.

Timothy Mack, president of the World Futures Society (Godbey, 2006) suggests three questions that need to be addressed as we contemplate the future and try to understand and plan for it.

1. How far ahead should you look in a practical sense?

This question very much depends on the variables that impact change and the issues to be addressed. Technology may be moving more quickly than economic change, so answers to questions related to technology might have a shorter "shelf life" than economic issues. Twenty years ago communities prepared 10- and 20-year master plans. Today, three to five years may seem a long-range projection. However, some of the broad structural issues in community planning such as subdivision and transportation planning need long-term vision, while the specifics and details of the plan need current and up-to-date strategies.

2. Where should you look for the future?

Once again this may depend on the issue being examined, but Mack suggests that we look beyond the traditional external data sets and include an examination of the internal dynamics of the organization that will shed light on the capacity to deal with change. In fact, the planning process outlined in this book is structured to examine the internal and external factors that effect change and the impact these issues will have on problem solving and decision making.

3. What should you look at?

Planning and problem solving rely on information from all available sources relevant to the issue to be considered. To rely on one data set without triangulating and validating the information with other data sets provides a narrow perspective on issues and could result in flawed decision making.

As an example, some recreation planners base their conclusions exclusively on survey research as though public opinion was all that mattered. While public opinion is important, other factors such as demographic change, consumer behavior, supply and use of existing services, and economic conditions also play a role. The short answer to this question is that all factors affecting change are important. The challenge is to give the right weight or importance to the influence of each factor so the overall impact can be accurately assessed.

5.4 Techniques for Forecasting

Once the required data sets have been defined and the information collected, there are any number of statistical models that can be applied to provide an analysis of the data. The analysis model chosen will vary depending on the type of data available and the accuracy of the prediction needed. For example, weather predictions are complex and can be based on a number of environmental factors affecting climate. They can also be based on the average temperature on a given day over time and are likely to be accurate within a reasonable margin of error. Predicting the number of golfers likely to use a course from year to year is extremely difficult. Weather is a major factor affecting play, so many course operators use five-year averages of past participation to develop predictions for use in a given year and develop their budgets accordingly.

There are techniques that are frequently used for forecasting and predicting future events. One is known as environmental scanning, and it involves an ongoing analysis of a variety of sources to detect signals of change that impact organizational development and decision making. The scan can be related to internal information scanning, external environmental scanning, or both. When change occurs, plans must be reviewed to ensure that the data and assumptions they were based on are still accurate and relevant.

Another approach is called trends analysis and extrapolation. This process involves collecting information related to planning and decision making and undertaking a content analysis of the data to determine factors relevant to the issues in question. Trends can be tracked in any number of areas including demographic and socioeconomic indicators, frequency and intensity of recreation participation, and attitudes and interests. One approach used by trends analysts is to monitor the headlines of newspapers across North America and undertake a content analysis of the information to illustrate forces of change.

One other method of forecasting uses focus groups or experts in targeted areas to develop probable future scenarios and test them for reliability and probability. This alternative future scenario-building approach is usually based on a best case/worst case approach with the highest degree of probability falling somewhere in the middle.

5.5 Trends in Leisure Programs and Facilities

There have been dramatic changes in the delivery of leisure service programs and facilities over the past three decades. Some of the changes have been evolutionary and some might be considered revolutionary. It is acknowledged that if we are going to understand how the future will unfold, it is important to understand the past. This requires that planners examine the underlying causes of change so that they can better anticipate how change will occur and predict the impact it will have. When change occurs, it is likely that a number of forces have worked together to bring that change about. Therefore, it is important that planners drill down to the root cause of change rather than accepting superficial explanations or rationales.

For example, there has been a major decline in physical activity among children and youth in our country. This decline could be because children today are less interested in physical activity, because there are fewer facilities available to accommodate programs, because there are no physical education programs in the schools, or because television and video games are more fun and appealing to children than a fitness class. If planners assume that the problem is related to a lack of facilities, they may recommend expensive strategies that do little to overcome the problem.

It is equally important that planners concentrate on the issues they can influence and develop appropriate strategies to affect change. If the real reason children are less active today is due to the influence of technology, then creative strategies, which acknowledge that influence, are needed. Technology isn't going away, so perhaps the solution is to incorporate technology into physical activity or at least ensure that physical activity is perceived to be as much fun as television and video games.

In reality, declining interest in physical activity may be related to all of the issues identified above. This emphasizes the point that problems are often based on a complex set of interrelated issues. Solutions therefore need to involve multiple strategies if problems are to be adequately addressed.

Following is a summary from the City of Brandon Recreation Facility Master Plan (2007) that identified recent trends affecting recreation development.

5.5.1 Facility Trends

Technology

Sport, recreation, and cultural facilities are going through a renaissance of sorts as the needs of consumers change and technology creates opportunities that previously didn't exist. It is now possible to swim in the winter in Canada and skate in the summer through technological innovation and design. Built environments allow us to create experiences we might not otherwise be able to have, and technology allows for virtual experiences that previously didn't exist, interactive communication, facility control systems, facility booking, and operating efficiencies.

Facility Development to Facility Maintaining

Communities across Canada have been faced with the dilemma of aging infrastructure, and a large percentage of public recreation facilities are well over twenty-five years old. Most communities did not create reserve accounts for facility replacement and are now faced with expensive retrofitting, renovation, and repair costs. Many of these facilities are also outdated to serve the changing recreation needs of the community.

Competitive Facilities to Leisure Amenities

Modern facilities concentrate on leisure amenities rather than competitive requirements. For example, the trend in leisure pool development serves a broader range of users and interests resulting in longer stays, increased revenue streams, and better service. Arenas are now adopting these concepts and integrating irregular "leisure ice surfaces" into their designs.

One Stop Service Centers

The new trend in facility development is to create one stop service centers or integrated, intergenerational facilities. These leisure malls are often developed in partnership with other service providers such as libraries, schools, and social service centers to capitalize on economies of scale, more efficient operation, lower impact facilities, and more convenience for the public.

The integrated leisure center complex also reflects another trend toward multipurpose spaces rather than dedicated, single activity space. This allows for more flexibility in use, and the components can be adapted to accommodate new activities as leisure needs change.

Green Facilities

With the increasing awareness of the environmental impact of major facility development, the trend is toward "green" facilities that are environmentally sensitive employing energy efficient design, low consumptive use, minimum impact on the community, reduced land use, and attractive aesthetic design to blend with the community. When new facilities are constructed, builders are encouraged to follow the LEED Canada (Leadership in Energy and Environmental Design) green building rating system which provides guidelines and standards for development and rates buildings according to established standards (certified, silver, gold, and platinum) for construction.

Recreation Facilities as Destinations

Many communities now recognize the value of recreation facilities as an economic generator. Unique, well-designed facilities can attract visitors and tourists who want to experience something different and will travel further to have these experiences. For example, the outdoor leisure pools in Winkler and Portage la Prairie attract visitors who travel to the community to experience something they don't have locally. The visit might include an overnight stay or visit to a restaurant. The Brandon Keystone Centre is an excellent example of a facility that could be considered a destination recreation facility catering to fairs, tournaments, sports events, and meetings. When contemplating the development of new facilities, opportunities should be explored to include unique amenities that would serve as an attraction.

Adaptive Reuse of Recreation Facilities

A new trend in recreation facility development is the adaptive reuse of existing spaces. Underutilized squash courts become climbing walls or yoga spaces and curling rinks or arenas become indoor soccer facilities. This approach is an economical way to develop a facility to meet new demands without the expense of new construction. Care must be taken too ensure that the planned use of the facility doesn't represent too great a compromise in the real needs of the facility users, and safety standards and playability requirements must be taken into consideration.

5.5.2 Program and Activity Trends

Recreation participation patterns and preferences affect the demand for and supply of recreation facilities. There are both internal and external activity trends that need to be considered when contemplating changes in the supply of facilities locally. The challenge is to be able predict with some accuracy the sustainability of activities over time and avoid the "build it and they will come" approach. Balancing the needs of competing interests and groups is extremely difficult when multimillion dollar facilities are at stake. The challenge for local governments is to balance the demands of special interest groups against the overall recreation facility needs of the community.

Changes in participation rates in local programs signal that facility use might change. Innovation in program and facility design occurring outside the community may eventually have an impact on facility development locally. The other challenge for local governments is to define what their goals and responsibilities are for facility development and move with caution to ensure sustainability of facilities that are developed.

There are many activity trends that will have an effect on facility use now and in the future.

David Foote (1996), in his analysis of predicted growth in sports partici-

Activity	% Growth	Rank
Hockey	2.36	8
Downhill Skiing	5.05	5
Swimming	5.55	3
Golf	7.01	2
Baseball	2.76	7
Cross-country	7.34	1
Volleyball	3.33	6
Tennis	5.21	4
Source: David K. Foot, 1996		

Table 5.1 Growth in Sports Participation, 1996–2001

pation between 1996–2001, found that of eight activities, hockey was predicted to have the lowest growth rate (2.36%) and cross-country skiing was predicted to have the highest (7.34%). While this fact alone shouldn't discourage communities from developing hockey facilities, it does raise issues about participation and facility development that need to be examined.

Program Planning Issues

The focus on program planning and development has shifted from program based to benefit based planning. Recreation program planning used to take the form of the cafeteria approach to choose where many programs were offered, and demand was measured on the basis of registration levels. Today, planners research and anticipate the benefits people seek from recreation participation and ensure that these benefits are available in the program design.

Accumulated to Targeted Services

Municipal governments recognize that with limited resources, they can't be all things to all people. Several decades ago, the approach was to try to offer everything and accumulate services. Today, priorities are set and core services defined to ensure that people with the greatest need receive the services they require. Most local governments target basic services to people who would not otherwise be served and leave more sophisticated recreation activities to the private sector. Defining what core services will be supported is the challenge for program planners.

Fitness to Health and Wellness

The trend in physical activity programming is on health-related outcomes rather than on narrow measures of fitness. In this approach, improved health through fitness is the objective rather than fitness as the end product. Improved health can be achieved in a variety of ways, and it represents one of the critical benefits of engagement in recreation.

Recent studies have highlighted the importance of physical activity in the lives of Canadians. Increases in sedentary lifestyles, growth in spectator and computer/ TV viewing, limited exercise opportunities in the school system, poor nutrition, and the growing cost of participation have resulted in what some refer to as a healthcare crisis for our youth. Increases in obesity and Type 2 diabetes are well-documented.

What is surprising is that a recent study (Gardiner, 2007) indicated that while only 10% of Manitoba children and teens get the recommended amount of daily physical activity, 94% of parents thought their kids got enough exercise. This gap between perception and reality illustrates the task ahead. The health of Canadians is everyone's problem, and solutions will not come from one source. Municipalities have an important role to play in that they provide facilities, leadership, and opportunity.

The Canadian Fitness and Lifestyle Research Institute recently released the results of a study (2004) that examined aspects related to local policy and the creation of supportive social and physical environments to promote physical activity among residents. It provides useful suggestions regarding the important role of municipalities in dissemination of information, support to targeted groups, program development, low-cost facility alternatives, transportation initiatives, subsidies for low-income residents, facility access, and creative partnerships.

"When asked about the number one thing they could do to improve their health, 80% of Canadians say they should be more physically active" (Physical Activity: for the Health of Canadians, 2002), and over 50% of Canadians intend to be more active, a strong predictor of future behavior. When they do, it is unlikely they will look to facilities such as arenas to meet their needs. They will, however, look to local governments and community support systems for help.

Team Sport to Lifetime Individual Pursuits

Over the past twenty years, there has been a real shift from team sport to life sport activities. Recent surveys that track the participation patterns of Canadians all report that the trend has been away from organized, structured recreation toward individual life sport activities.

Indoor to Outdoor Focus

Another trend in participation is from a focus on indoor activities to outdoor pursuits. While we rely on indoor facilities for many activities because we live in a cold climate country, outdoor pursuits have become very popular. There has been an increase in use and popularity of the skating ovals, cycling, walking, and cross-country ski trail systems, and snowmobile areas.

Over the past ten years, survey after survey (CFLRI, 2000) of participation preferences have identified walking, gardening, hiking, home

	Rank 2000	Rank 1996	Rank 1992	Rank 1988	Rank 1981
Walking for pleasure	1	1	1	2	6
Golf	2	2	3	3	2
Camping	3	3	2	1	1
Bicycling	4	n/a	4	6	15
Craft/Hobby	5	10	10	8	n/a
Gardening	6	8	27	13	26
Swimming	7	6	6	5	8
Read books/magazines	8	5	7	7	7
Hiking/backpacking	9	13	16	19	23
Fishing	10	4	5	4	4
Running/jogging	11	9	21	25	16
Downhill skiing/snowboarding	12	14	17	11	3
Performing arts	13	32	19	37	n/a
Ice hockey	14	27	8	9	5
Aerobic/fitness/aquasize	15	7	11	12	n/a
Softball/baseball	16	11	9	14	12
Curling	17	17	12	10	10
Soccer	18	29	n/a	54	35
Dancing	19	16	13	18	13
Hunting/shooting	20	20	15	16	11
TV/movies	20	31	n/a	41	21

Source: A Look at Leisure #41 (2000)

Table 5.2 Favorite Recreation Activities (1981–2000)

exercise, swimming, social dance, bicycling, golf, and other outdoor pursuits in the top ten.

The implication for local governments is to focus on ensuring the availability of trails, parks, and open spaces and focus less on indoor arenas and single-purpose facilities.

Risk and Adventure Recreation

Combined with the interest in outdoor recreation is a growth in risk or adventure recreation, activities such as skateboarding, snowboarding, climbing, and mountain biking. These activities are important areas to nurture because they work so well with programs for youth at risk and those not interested in organized and regulated activities.

6.0 Demographics and Community Profiles

6.1 Introduction to Demographics and Community Profiles

Demographics are described as a wide range of population characteristics and variables that can include age, gender, income, marital status, employment, education, length of residence, ethnicity, place of residence, and household composition. Socioeconomic status refers to specific variables of income, education, and occupation. A demographic analysis should not only include information about the current status and make-up of the community but also predictions about population growth and socioeconomic status that are important factors in community planning.

A community profile is used to identify demographic variables and population characteristics in a specific geographical area for the purpose of interpretation and comparative analysis. Many communities prepare profiles to explain the nature of their community, to market and promote the community, to encourage business relocation, to attract new residents, and to track the changing nature of the community for planning purposes. In addition to demographic and socioeconomic data, community profiles include factors such as employment levels and opportunities, community economic status and affordability, industrial diversification, tax base, community institutions and infrastructure, climate, cultural and ethnic make-up, and other "quality of life" information.

6.2 Significance of Demographics

Demographics and population characteristics are extremely important factors in understanding current behavior and predicting future events. David Foot (1996) believes that "demographics explains about two-thirds of everything" and he uses this belief to explain how changing population characteristics will impact on social change, consumer behavior, and economic shifts over time.

Some demographic factors are quite easy to recognize, understand, and predict. The post-war baby boom, as an example, has had a profound social, economic, and cultural impact on communities and institutions as it worked its way through the population pyramid affecting everything from construction of new schools to consumer spending. Other demo-

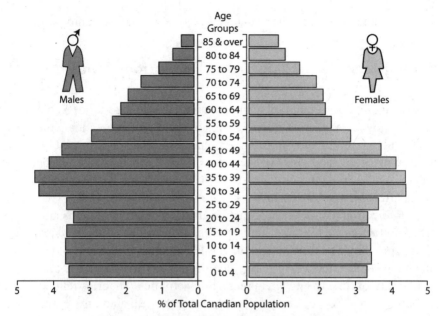

Figure 6.1 (% of Total Canadian Population)

(Source: Canada. Statistics Canada. 1996 Census of Population)

graphic changes are less dramatic, and resulting change can be subtle and harder to predict and detect.

Regardless of the magnitude, demographic change has a profound impact on society and communities. Understanding how these changes affect community is central to successful planning and appropriate community development. Observing signals of change by monitoring the Population Pyramid (Figure 6.1) and other sources of demographic data is a key responsibility of planners. Studying visual graphs, charts, and illustrations like Figure 6.1 speaks volumes about demographic change and the impact it is likely to have on communities and institutions.

Some of the best sources for population information are Statistics Canada (www.statcan.ca/), which conducts the Canadian census, and the Province of Manitoba.

The Province of Manitoba has developed a web site with access to community profiles for all Manitoba communities. This site provides the most comprehensive profile information for every community and region in Manitoba. Each community profile offers up-to-date information covering everything from location (maps) to quality of life indicators (demographics, population, labor force, education, history, recreational facilities) to economic indicators (utilities, transportation, taxation, land, buildings, and development). It can be found at www.communityprofiles. mb.ca/.

6.3 Impact of Demographics on Recreation Planning

Understanding the demographic characteristics and make-up of a community and how these factors might change over time is an essential component in planning. An accurate demographic analysis identifies the types of users, consumers, and clients you work with and how their age, gender, income, education, ethnicity, proximity to services, and past experiences might affect their use of facilities, programs, and services.

Recreation planners know that leisure participation patterns are based on factors such as age, gender, ethnicity, marital status, physical ability, proximity to service, and disposable income. Economic and employment status affects disposable income, and marital status can affect availability of time to engage in recreation activities. Theories related to "leisure through the life cycle" explain a great deal about the participation patterns of people as they age and how participation is affected during childbearing years. The program interests of participants are influenced greatly by ethnicity, cultural background, and past experiences.

Understanding these factors and the make-up of the community will facilitate appropriate program development, accurate target marketing, realistic measures of consumption, and sustainable facility development. Neighborhood profiles will also contribute to decisions regarding the strategic location and accessibility of services and realistic user fees and charges.

6.4 Issues and Limitations Related to Demographic Profiling

While demographics represent an important source of information for planners, care must be taken to ensure that the use of this data is balanced with other important community planning factors. Stereotyping must be avoided by recognizing that demographics represent norms and averages that may not apply or be relevant in every situation.

It is equally important to ensure that demographic analysis and population distribution by percentages are not used to misrepresent situations. For example, a 15% increase in population of seniors in a community of 10,000 people might seem quite dramatic. However, if the actual number of seniors in the community is 450, then 15% represents an increase of 67 residents. While this change in the demographic make-up of

Figure 7.1 Maslow's Hierarchy of Needs
(Source: Maslow's Hierarchy of Needs Abraham Maslow, Motivation and
Personality, 2nd ed. Harper & Row, 1970)

the community is important, it must be taken in context and considered in
light of other demographic changes occurring in the community.

7.0 Demand Analysis and Public Consultation

7.1 Introduction

An important factor in determining recreation facility requirements is
to understand what consumers and participants want. There is considerable confusion about what constitutes "need" and how to most accurately
measure it. There are also a number of approaches to consider when consulting with the community in an attempt to better understand their interests, aspirations, needs, demands, and requirements.

The following section attempts to provide some clarity regarding the definitions of need and demand as well as an overview of the process involved in meaningful public consultation.

7.2 Need and Demand

Recreation planners frequently use the terms "needs assessment" and "demand analysis" interchangeably. In fact, need and demand have distinct meanings, and it can be misleading to assume they are synonymous.

7.2.1 Need Defined

Needs are the things that people can't do without. The hierarchy of needs developed by Maslow (see Figure 7.1 in Maslow (1970) from www. drugby.co.uk) suggests that lower order needs (physiological) must be satisfied before higher order needs (self-actualization) can be satisfied. This should prompt planners to assess carefully the profile of the community they are dealing with so that they can understand what motivates use and consumption of service. While there may be an argument that recreation can play a role in each of the five categories of needs defined by Maslow, it is generally believed that recreation is more closely associated with social, esteem, and self-actualization needs. Basic human needs are driven by survival instinct, and until the basic needs for food, shelter, clothing, and safety are met, it is unlikely that people will address their higher order needs. Basic human needs are affected by cultural, social, and economic circumstances, and in this regard, it is important to distinguish between the things we need to survive and the things that enhance quality of life.

7.2.2 Demand Defined

Essentially, demand is an expression of the things we would like to have or are most likely to use if available.

Demand can be latent in the sense that participation can be constrained by many factors that, if removed, would stimulate and increase use. For example, the cost of a public swim ticket might present a barrier for some people, but if the price were discounted this constraint would be removed, making it possible to participate. Demand can also be induced or stimulated by creative marketing. Participation and use is affected by knowledge and perception of the service. Creative marketing can induce participation by making people aware of a service or presenting it in a completely different light than they previously perceived it to be.

7.2.3 Measuring Demand

With respect to sport and recreation facility development, accurately determining current and future demand is critical to the planning process. Measuring what people want or would like to have in the future is described as demand analysis.

Demand is influenced by a number of factors and measured using various data collection techniques. The factors can include:

- Cost versus perceived benefit
- Use and consumption
- New trends
- Proximity to the facility (time/distance)
- Profile of potential users
- Needs assessment
- Time

1. Cost versus Perceived Benefit

Economic theories about pricing suggest that as the price of something goes up, demand will decrease. This is known as the elasticity of demand, and price is one of the well-established constraints or barriers to participation. The relationship between price and perceived benefit is also important to understand because if the outcome (benefit) doesn't reflect price, consumers will look elsewhere.

This is particularly true in a competitive marketplace where consumers have choice and factors such as quality of the facility and customer service influence user decisions. It is well-documented that facility users will bypass a facility perceived to be of poorer quality and travel farther distances to use higher-quality facilities, and might pay higher fees to go there.

2. Use or Consumption

Tracking use, participation rates, and repeat visits provides a measure of current demand. It establishes the willingness of the public to participate, and both the frequency and intensity of participation should be measured. This is accomplished by keeping accurate records of registration levels and waiting lists to see where demand is met or where an oversupply or inadequate supply of facilities and services exists. Accurately measuring the capacity of the facility or program versus consumption is an important element of this analysis.

3. New Trends-Comparative Analysis

Tracking facility use patterns and undertaking a comparative analysis with similar facilities in another geographic location is useful in predicting likely participation rates in your facility. It can also provide information about potential demand for a facility not presently available in your community. An evaluation of current participation rates against the "program life cycle" is another means to track trends in the popularity of programs and facilities and predict the likelihood they will continue.

4. Location and Proximity (Time/Distance)

Demand and frequency of facility use can be driven by the proximity of users to the service or facility. The closer that users are to the facility, the greater frequency with which they are likely to use the service. Location is a critical factor in determining demand and use of service.

5. Profile of Potential Users

Demand is driven by socioeconomic, cultural, and demographic characteristics. Factors such age, gender, marital status, and disposable income all impact on leisure participation throughout the life cycle and are useful predictors of program participation and facility demand. An analysis of the profile of community residents relative to demographic and socioeconomic trends will provide the basis for planners to predict demand for programs and facilities demands in the future.

6. Needs Assessment and Public Consultation

Perhaps the most important aspect of demand analysis is for facility planners to ask the public for their input. Public consultation involves various strategies to determine need and demand. One of these strategies is community needs assessment utilizing survey research. Public consultation strategies and survey research are dealt with in detail in section 7.3.

7. Time

The most frequent response to questions about barriers to participation is time. When asked about fitness participation, some people indicate they don't have enough time to participate. Time diaries are useful tools in understanding how people actually use their time. Time diary analysis shows that on average, one third of our time is discretionary where we are free to decide how to spend that time. When people say they don't have time for fitness, what they really mean is that they have other priorities. Understanding how people spend their discretionary time is an important consideration in facility planning and development.

7.3 Public Consultation

— *7.3.1 Introduction*

Participatory democracy through public consultation is now considered to be standard practice in the process of facility development. Whether it is a public, commercial, or not-for-profit facility, the members, users, and local citizens expect to be consulted, and to avoid this step in the process would seriously compromise the end result.

Public consultation is complex and not without its limitations. The challenge for planners is to design a process that is both meaningful to the participants and helpful to the planning process. Public consultation is not limited to soliciting opinions and reaction; it is also a process to generate current user data, demographic profiles, user perceptions, expectations, opinions, attitudes, and ideas.

— *7.3.2 Benefits of Public Consultation*

Public consultation provides an opportunity for planners to better inform the public and resolve conflicts as they arise. It is easier to address issues as the process evolves than to fix things or convince people once the process is completed. Some of the other benefits are that the process can be used to test ideas and alternatives, set priorities, achieve consensus, and rally support for the initiative.

— *7.3.3 Three Steps to Meaningful Public Participation*

There are many strategies and creative approaches to consultation that can lead to meaningful public participation. Some types of public consultation work better in some situations and with some groups than with others. The challenge for planners is to select the right approach for a given situation and ensure that it is executed successfully.

The three steps in the process of public consultation involve first identifying who should be consulted, then the level of involvement required, and finally selection of the consultation strategy best suited to the task.

Step 1. Who Should be Consulted?

This is an important question to address at the outset of any project. It is important to be inclusive, but equally important to be practical and efficient. Frequently, in public recreation planning exercises, elected officials want all citizens to have a say through a community survey or consultation process. A survey of all residents might meet political objectives, but isn't necessary from a planning perspective, because valid and reliable information can be collected from a representative sample, thereby reducing the time and cost associated with the exercise. The tendency to want to involve everyone can bog the process down and paralyze decision making.

One rule of thumb is to consult anyone who will be affected by the issue or plan as well as stakeholders who might have an effect on the plan. The "public" to be consulted could include individuals, special interest groups, business community representatives, competing or partner agencies, and other communities of interest.

Step 2. Level of Involvement—From Information to Empowerment

The level of involvement in the planning process, from information sharing to empowerment, represents the degree of power transferred from authorities to the public. As the level of communication and involvement increases, so does the degree of responsibility for the outcome. While empowerment is a desirable objective, it may not be practical or desirable in every situation. While citizen input is useful and important, care must be taken to ensure that it is accurate, reliable, and valid. Professional expertise and judgement may also be required to ensure appropriate decision making.

Striking the right balance between informing and empowering is challenging, because transferring authority and responsibility at the appropriate time will impact greatly on the success of the plan.

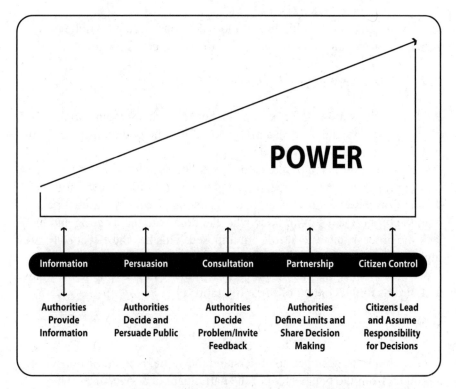

Figure 7.3 Citizen Participation and Decision Making
(Adapted From: Lutzin (1980). Managing Municipal Leisure Services p. 276.)

Figure 7.3 illustrates the consultation continuum and the degree of control, authority, and responsibility that is transferred as public involvement is increased.

Step 3. Strategy for Consultation

The third step in the process of public consultation is to select the most appropriate approach that will complement the planning process and issues being addressed.

Individuals and community groups have different motives for involvement in the planning process. Some have a genuine interest in making the community a better place to live and their ideas have merit. Some are motivated solely by self-interest and may try to dominate or subvert the consultation process for their own benefit. The consultation process should focus on strategies that minimize bias and maximize broad-based public input. Recognizing the strengths and limitations of each approach to public consultation will be helpful in selecting one that will work best in a given situation. It is likely that more than one strategy will be necessary if the broad interests of the public are to be accurately reflected.

A. Public Meetings – Open Forums

Public meetings or open forums can be held at strategic points in the planning process and used as a means to inform the public, increase public awareness, and invite feedback.

The limitations to public meetings are that attendance is open, interest groups can stack the meeting, and the time available can limit the depth of discussion. As a result, public meetings frequently attract people with the biggest stake in an issue who can dominate the meeting and hijack the process unless controls are imposed. This has the effect of limiting debate, and the views of the "silent majority" often go unheard. The process has merit, but planners must weigh the results of public meetings and forums in the context of these limitations.

B. Focus Groups

Focus groups are designed to understand the value, benefit, or impact of a product from the perspective of the participant or service user. They differ from workshops in that they are a structured research process to collect qualitative information in a controlled setting using specific research techniques. Focus groups are extremely useful tools in the planning process in that they meaningfully engage participants, fully explore issues, ideas, and alternatives, generate feedback, and gain a perspective not otherwise possible.

C. Community Workshops

Workshops can take on many forms but their intent is to bring together interested parties to explore issues in-depth and facilitate inclusion in the planning process. They can also be a method of information sharing to test ideas and receive feedback and are often less structured than focus groups, but allow the freedom to probe issues.

Nominal grouping is an example of a facilitated collaborative process used to develop consensus on issues and identify priorities. The process encourages full participation by all present and everyone has an equal say.

The PATH Process (Figure 7.4) is another technique to engage a large number of people in a meaningful consultation process. PATH is

Figure 7.4 PATH Process
(Source: Ashuk, B., 2000, City of Winnipeg)

an acronym for Planning Alternative Tomorrows with Hope and involves both a graphic recorder and a process facilitator.

Simulation, role-playing, and scenario building are some other examples of group process used to explore issues, ideas, and problem-solving strategies. The approach used is to engage in role-playing where participants act out various scenarios to see what the consequences of various options might be and determine whether better alternatives exist.

All of these workshop strategies are designed to delve more deeply into issues, generate alternative solutions, and examine their impact in an effort to choose the most appropriate solution.

D. Media or Promotional Displays

Shopping mall displays, information open houses, and drop-in consultation are means to engage people in the planning process informally and allow for an exchange of ideas with planners. This approach is useful in avoiding "grandstanding" that can occur at a public meeting, usually for the benefit of the local news media. It also allows planners to provide information to the general public, receive feedback, and probe the public for ideas and alternatives.

E. Interviews

Conducting interviews with communities of interest (special interest groups) or the public can be extremely useful in generating valuable insight into issues and getting qualitative and anecdotal information. While special interest groups have a bias toward the cause they represent, no one likely knows their needs and issues better than representatives from the organization. They can provide detail about their users and programs and services they provide as well as a rationale for new initiatives and ideas.

Interviews with the public or key community informants can provide insight from what might be considered the "silent majority" who wouldn't otherwise be consulted. The limitation of this process is that it is extremely time-consuming and expensive. Care must also be taken to factor in bias that might exist and other forms of research employed to validate the findings and perspectives gained from interviews.

F. Panel of Experts

Complex planning projects often require professional expertise from a number of different perspectives. Establishing a project steering committee with expertise in targeted areas can generate high-quality solutions and improve the success of a plan. One of the limitations of using experts and professionals is that they can intimidate the general public who may feel their ideas and suggestions will be ridiculed or criticized. The challenge is to combine professional expertise with the views of the public and users so that a balanced view emerges.

G. Written Briefs

Written briefs are another way to invite the public and communities of interest to submit position papers related to the issues in question. They provide an opportunity for anyone in the community to have input into the planning process and can generate facts, statistics, trends, opinions, and attitudes from user groups that can be helpful to planners. Again, bias can be reflected in these submissions, so planners must use briefs in the context in which they are presented.

H. Market Research

Market and survey research are some of the public consultation tools available to planners. It is a primary process of data and information gathering either from a defined population or a sample of the population. It is used to identify attitudes, behavior, knowledge, opinions, and demographic information. It is, however, a complex process and is dealt with in more detail in the section to follow.

Combined Consultation Process

The previous section outlined eight unique methods to consult with the public. Each method has advantages and disadvantages, but none of these approaches on its own will provide the broad perspective of public opinion necessary. Using several of them in combination will allow planners to validate information they gather from one source with data from another and allow for the triangulation of data.

7.4 Conducting Survey Research

As indicated earlier, survey research is a complex but important primary data collection process. The types of information typically collected in a survey include:

a. Behavior

A survey can find out what activities people say they are engaging in and the frequency and intensity of use. Knowledge of current participation patterns is an excellent predictor of future use and behavior.

b. Knowledge

Surveys help determine the level of knowledge and understanding about available programs, facilities, and services and can probe the respondent for perceptions of quality and quantity of these services.

c. Attitudes

Surveys measure public attitudes and opinions and assist in identifying issues that need to be addressed, and the response the public is likely to have to various solutions.

d. Demographic and Socioeconomic Status

Questions regarding age, gender, income, ethnicity, marital status, and education are used to better understand the context in which the respondent is answering and to validate information collected by other consultation strategies.

The value and benefit of survey research is that it can provide information from the "silent majority" both efficiently and effectively, provided that it is conducted in an objective and scientific manner. If survey research is managed scientifically, it can provide valid and reliable data from a small sample of the population that can be generalized to the entire population with accuracy. This can make it both an economical and efficient tool for planners.

The limitation of survey research is that, if not managed scientifically, the process can be manipulated and it is subject to bias and perceptions that are open to interpretation.

Steps in the Process

There are five steps in the process of survey research that are each equally important if the survey is to achieve its intended purpose. It is not the intent of this planning book to provide details of the survey research process, but rather to outline an approach and identify resources available (Dilman, 2007) to assist in the process should they be needed.

Step 1. Determine Survey Objectives

The first step is to be clear about the purpose, focus, use, and intent of the survey. If the goals are unclear, the results will lack clarity. Understanding what information is needed and how the information will be used is an important component of survey design. If these issues are not thought out carefully, the answers to questions will have limited use to planners.

Step 2. Establish Sample

Deciding whom to sample is one of the biggest issues in every survey. When a community undertakes a survey, elected officials frequently want to give everyone a chance to be heard. While this may meet political objectives, it is neither practical nor necessary from a scientific perspective. Selecting a random sample that is representative of the overall population will assure the validity of the results.

There are two types of random sampling. One is probability sampling, where everyone in the population has an equal chance of being selected in the sample through a scientific process. This approach avoids bias and ensures that the sample is representative of the population.

Nonprobability sampling is less scientific and not everyone in the population has a chance of being selected. Surveys that are handed out randomly at a shopping mall, left in a public place, or distributed through the local daily paper are nonprobability samples because they eliminate people who do not shop in the mall or don't subscribe to the local paper. This approach can generate useful information but it isn't representative of the population, can't be generalized beyond the sample collected, and has a built-in response bias.

Step 3. Construct and Test Survey

Constructing a survey is a challenging and difficult process. So many factors need to be considered because they affect everything from response rates to the validity and reliability of the results. The appearance of the survey affects people's perception of the value of the exercise. It is known, for example, that the color of paper used for the survey affects return rates. The time of day for phone surveys and the scheduling of mail-out distribution are also factors that affect response rates. It is critical that the survey be clearly worded and that instructions are easily understood. Avoid jargon and be both precise and concise in the wording of questions. The order that questions appear in is an important consideration, and it is believed that the easiest questions to complete should be asked first. The easiest questions are demographic and socioeconomic questions, followed by participation information.

Distribution			
Performance	**Mail Out**	**Telephone**	**Door/Door**
Cost	Low	Medium	High
Time	Slow	Fast	Medium
Information	Low	High	High

Table 7.1 Comparative Survey Distribution Techniques

The key to every survey is to do a pre-test to work out any problems and refine the appearance, timing, instructions, and clarity of the questions prior to fielding the survey.

Step 4. Distribution Methodology

There are several acceptable methods used to conduct and distribute surveys. Each method has its own benefits and limitations, so a judgement must be made about which method will suit the purpose, timing, and budget of the agency conducting the survey. The key factors to weigh when choosing a distribution method involve the cost of distribution, the time and resources involved, and the quality of information gained from the survey (Table 7.1).

The most common methods are mail-out and telephone surveys. There are other variations on these survey methodologies, including interviewer completed techniques such as door-to-door and shopping mall surveys.

Mail-out surveys (Dilman,1978) can be less costly than phone surveys but are more time-consuming and difficult to field and tabulate. The phone survey can be fielded very quickly and provide better qualitative information in that the participants can be probed for clarity of responses, but are more expensive to field.

Step 5. Analysis and Interpretation

The last step in the process is the tabulation of results and the analysis and interpretation of the answers. The raw data tell a story, but using graphs and charts to illustrate the significance of the results is an important component, the planning and reporting process. It is important that professionals knowledgeable about the issues raised in the survey are involved in the analysis or the results can be misleading.

8.0 Standards

8.1 Introduction Standards

Standards are generally accepted principles, criteria or specifications that are often used to guide planning and decision making. They are developed to regulate public health and safety, improve quality and consistency, and provide measures for comparative analysis to help judge the merits and effectiveness of facility developments.

Standards can be either voluntary or imposed. Those that are enforced for health and safety reasons, or to guarantee accessibility, are generally developed and passed into law by federal, provincial, and local governments or regulatory authorities such as the Canadian Safety Standards Association (CSA). Standards that regulate bathing loads in pools, circulation space for patrons, restricted smoking areas, and safe playground equipment are examples of legislated standards.

Voluntary standards are established to improve quality of experience, ensuring that there is adequate space for an activity and that users can comfortably participate. These are often established by facility planners or others who prepare guidelines for space allocation. The American College of Sports Medicine (1997) has established recommended standards for health and fitness facilities. For example, they recommend a minimum of 20 to 25 square feet of space for each person using a fitness floor at any one time. This standard should ensure that patrons could participate in an activity comfortably and get more enjoyment out of the experience without feeling crowded.

Some standards are set by authorities that govern the rules and regulations associated with various activities. They specify the space requirements and conditions required for the activity and dictate how facility design and development must be done to accommodate it. These types of standards are developed to ensure that an activity (sport) will be performed in space that is consistent from one facility to another so that performances can be compared.

Most international sport-governing bodies require that the specifications for high-performance sport facilities be consistent everywhere in the world. Facilities are inspected regularly to ensure that they conform to these standards, or world record performances will not be recognized. Facility requirements and standards differ for various age groups and levels of competition. It is cost prohibitive to build every rink, pool, court, and diamond to international specification, so for practical reasons, the

Component	Low	High
Arena Enclosure	Plywood Boards	Plexi-glass
Pool Enclosure	Flat 6 Lane 20m Pool	Leisure/Wave Pool
Golf Enclosure	Greens - Weekly Cut	Greens - Cut Daily
Tennis Courts	3" Base/Asphalt Surface	8" Base/Laycold Surface
Football Field	Grass Turf	Artificial Turf
Fitness Studio	1" Treadmill/50 persons	1 Treadmill/20 persons

Table 8.1 Qualitative Facility Standards

standards used in the development of sport facilities should match the intended level of play.

Another type of standard is one used to measure current supply against best practices in the industry. Often these types of standards are based on industry norms for communities, service centers, or organizations of a similar size and are used as a basis for comparison. For example, if Winnipeg has one indoor arena for every 30,000 population and Calgary has one for every 20,000, then Winnipeg's supply of arenas could be judged substandard.

Planners acknowledge that the supply and availability of facilities should be based on community-specific circumstances rather than what other communities have. However, standards do provide a useful planning tool if they are used in conjunction with other factors and indicators, rather than as an isolated measure to justify development decisions.

8.2 Definitions and Typology of Standards

Standards generally fall into two categories, qualitative and quantitative. Both types are equally important but serve different purposes.

Qualitative Standards

Qualitative standards involve issues such as accessibility, safety, cleanliness, and comfort that affect the quality of the participants' experience (e.g., regulations governing emergency equipment, access for the disabled, and professional supervision of high-risk areas). Other types of qualitative standards are voluntary but affect the competitive edge a facility might realize. The quality of the facility is judged by the level of finishing and furnishings, space allocation, and the quality of the environment for the activity. It is generally believed that private clubs are developed to a higher-standard with higher-quality amenities than public facilities.

When applying qualitative standards to facility development, many factors must be taken into consideration. Some of the variables include the level of play to be accommodated, the expectations of the users, the capital budget available for development, and the priorities for allocation of financial resources. There are also standards, guidelines, and legislation concerning barrier-free design that require facilities be built so that they are fully accessible, and all facilities are expected to adhere to these functional standards.

Quantitative

Quantitative standards refer to the number of facilities and amenities and the amount of equipment available to serve the user. For example, quantitative standards can include the number of gyms, courts, fields, and fitness centers per population level, equipment stations per user, and parking stalls per square feet of facility.

One method of defining quantitative standards is the population ratio method, where the total park space or the number of facilities available are described on the basis of the size of the population to be served. A common standard applied to open space acquisition and development is 10 acres per 1,000 population. It is a rule of thumb that municipalities use when contemplating new subdivisions and in their land use policies. It reflects a measure of the amount of land needed to accommodate outdoor recreation spaces on a basis of population and is useful in that it is sensitive to density of development. In high-density developments, the land needed can be expanded as the density grows.

The population ratio method applies to facilities rather than park space and is described in terms of the number of facilities per population. For example, in Winnipeg there are currently 13 indoor pools or 1 pool / 53,000 persons. There are also 72 community centers, so the population ratio is approximately 1 / 9,000 persons.

A second type of quantitative standard is defined as area percentage. This standard refers to the amount of space allocated for parks and recreation purposes when land is developed or new subdivisions approved. Across Canada, the common practice is to require 10% of the developable land in new subdivisions to be set aside for parks and recreation purposes. This standard reflects an estimate of the minimum amount of space needed to meet local recreation and park needs within reasonable proximity to the users.

While this can serve as a guideline, the area percentage standard is not sensitive to the density of the development. For example, in a high-rise apartment complex, very high population densities can be achieved, and the 10% land dedication may not be adequate to meet the needs of the population. In addition, communities are often tempted to accept cash from the land developer in lieu of land dedication. This is driven by the need to have money to develop recreation facilities, but later, communities can find themselves without adequate land to meet local needs.

8.3 Principles and Practices in the Implementation of Standards

Generally, standards are used as a tool to assess the extent to which the needs of people are being met. Once they are established, the supply of existing facilities can be measured against standards to determine deficiencies or identify where an oversupply exists, and corrective action can be taken.

Standards are just one of the tools available to planners and should never be a substitute for comprehensive planning. Some of the general principles to be kept in mind when defining standards are that they should be:

- Realistic and attainable
- Based on community specific characteristics
- Able to stand the test of time
- Agreed to or endorsed by policymakers
- Applied with caution

If standards are developed and used appropriately, they can assist in reducing the influence of special interest groups, distribute services equitably in the community, improve the quality of service, and achieve efficiency in facility development.

Applying standards too rigidly can be problematic. In large communities with multiple facilities, it is somewhat easier to plan on the basis of accepted industry standards. Many small communities will only build one arena, community center, theater, gymnasium, fitness center, or pool. Knowing when it is appropriate to develop these types of facilities is not a matter of national industry standards, but rather, local community needs and available resources.

There are many resources available that describe in detail the qualitative and quantitative standards that guide recreation facility development. The key is to ensure that the application of standards is suitable for the community or facility to which they are being applied.

8.4 Limitations of the Use of Standards in Planning

Standards have their limitations, particularly if they are not used appropriately. In some respects, standards can be seen as rigid and inflexible, reducing opportunities for creativity and unique developments. Frequently they are defined as "minimum standards" that, once established, limit opportunities to go beyond the minimum requirement or expectation. Standards should not be seen as absolutes or goals to achieve, but rather as guidelines to be applied with caution and considered in the light of other influencing factors.

Section IV
Synthesis, Analysis, and Reporting

9.0 Data Analysis and Interpretation

9.1 Introduction

This chapter deals with the most important step in the planning process where the data and information collected are analyzed and interpreted so that choices and decisions can be made and a plan developed to guide future actions.

Essentially, planning is an exercise in problem solving through the process of both creative and critical thinking that leads to sound decision making. On one hand, creative thinking requires a broadening of perspectives to consider all ideas, possibilities, and alternatives, while creative thinking involves an examination of ideas using a narrow focus and defined criteria to identify the most reasonable and logical idea or solution. Both approaches are useful and necessary in a comprehensive planning process, but when choices are necessary between two or more competing ideas, creative thinking, logic, and sound judgement is necessary.

Creative thinking and decision making can involve logic and intuitive thinking, but there is also a range of analytical tools available to guide the process and minimize bias in the process. Tools such as the critical path method (CPM), decision tree, and Gantt chart method are a means to add structure to the decision-making process.

The section that follows describes an eight-step approach to analysis, interpretation, and decision making and details the priority-criterion ranking system, an analytical model to facilitate critical thinking and decision making.

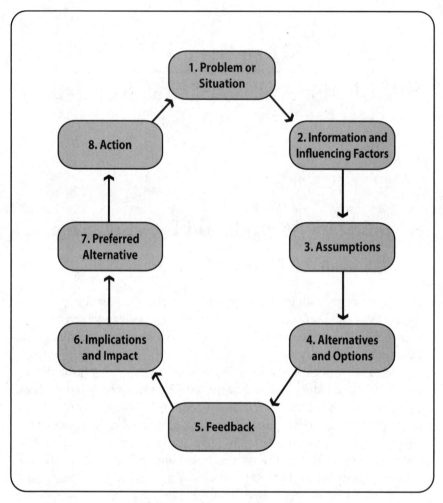

Figure 9.1 Eight-Step Approach to Decision Making

9.2 The Eight-Step Approach to Decision Making

The process of data analysis, interpretation, and decision making can be complex given that there may be multiple data sets and competing interests and objectives. The role of the planner is to objectively assess the information available and identify strategies that represent the most efficient and effective course of action within available resources. The key steps in the process are shown in Figure 9.1.

Step 1. Define the Problem, Issue, or Situation

The first step in the process is to accurately define the problem(s) that needs to be solved and the issues that relate to the problem. Failure to accurately define and understand the problem and the issues that need to be addressed could result in a flawed process and an unsatisfactory plan or resolution to the problem.

There is an old saying that "if you can't fix it with a hammer, you have an electrical problem." This emphasizes the need to clearly understand the scope of the problem before action is taken to fix it. For example, if the issue is declining use of racquetball/squash courts, a planner might conclude that the problem is related to diminishing interest in the activity and contemplate taking the courts out of service. Further examination might suggest that the real problem is the quality of the activity space, poor maintenance or poor customer service. The fix for each of these problems will require different solutions and removing the courts from service might be premature and unwarranted.

Creative thinking would contribute greatly to defining the problem accurately and comprehensively.

Step 2. Information, Data, and Factors

After the problem has been accurately defined, the next step is to identify what information and data will be needed to better understand the problem and the factors that will affect possible solutions.

It is important to understand the value and limitations of various forms of data and information. Essentially, information is facts organized in a useful way to facilitate clarity and understanding. There is both hard and soft data available that can be used to clarify issues.

Hard data is typically factual and statistical information based on scientific enquiry where rigor and controls are involved. This type of data is typically thought to be more valid, reliable, and precise. Examples of quantifiable data include census and demographic information, facility inventories, participation data, budget expenditures, and scientific surveys.

Soft data is often less quantifiable and difficult to validate. This type of information includes public opinion, attitudes, assumptions, and prediction of trends. The limitation of soft data is that bias can be present and minimize the validity and reliability of the information.

Both hard and soft data are important in developing a broad perspective on problems and issues, but care must be taken with respect to the significance attributed to the various forms of data used to make decisions.

More weight is usually given to hard data, and soft data needs to be validated through other forms of inquiry.

Sections II and III of this book outline the critical planning factors that will have an impact on planning decisions. These factors will vary in importance with the type of plan being developed and the problems being addressed. Factors such as goals for the project, inventory of existing facilities, capacity and use of services, demographic and socioeconomic conditions, trends, and standards will all affect the direction of a plan and problem-solving exercise. Information regarding all of these factors needs to be collected and examined in relation to the problems being addressed in the plan.

Step 3. Assumptions

At the beginning of the planning process, assumptions are made about a number of factors affecting the plan and decisions that need to be made. Assumptions are propositions and ideas that are, to a great extent, taken for granted or assumed to be true. Some assumptions can be validated through the planning process while others cannot. In the course of the planning and decision-making process, relevant information should be collected in an effort to test and validate assumptions, thereby strengthening the argument for or against a given issue.

Some examples of assumptions that might be made when contemplating the development of a new recreation facility might be:

- Fitness and physical activity will continue to increase in importance
- The population of the community will grow by 10% in the next year
- There is a deficiency of fitness facilities to serve the current population

If these assumptions proved to be correct, there could be an argument made for additional fitness facilities in the community. If they are inaccurate, new facilities for fitness might not be necessary.

Step 4. Alternatives and Options

At this stage in the decision-making process, all ideas and strategies should be identified and clearly expressed. This is the step where the data and information generated in the planning process is used to analyze the pros and cons of each option. The challenge for planners is that a number of equally appealing strategies may emerge, and decisions need to be made about the most appropriate course of action.

When options are being considered, it is important that all available information related to the issues is considered. Overemphasis of one type of information can flaw the decision-making process. For example, an overemphasis on public opinion may not provide the most valid and reliable information. It is important to "triangulate" several data sets to validate one against another. For example, if the public believes that a new pool is needed in the community, it will be useful to test this assumption against current supply and use, trends in pool use in the community over the past five years, standards of pool supply per person in other communities, and demographic variables of primary pool users.

Step 5. Feedback

One strategy to assist in sorting through a number of competing options is to consult with the stakeholders affected by the plan and the decisions that are being considered. Their feedback can be useful in measuring the implications and impact of various alternatives and gauging support for various options.

Step 6. Implication and Impact

An important factor to consider in the decision-making process is the short- and long-term implications and impact of each option. Each option will have an effect on who benefits from and who pays for the decision. In addition, it must be determined if there is sufficient support for the option to ensure that it is sustainable over the long term. The weight of the decision will be governed by the consequence of error and how much is at stake. Some decisions may have a profound impact on the community while others may be relatively neutral.

Step 7. Preferred Alternative—Feasibility versus Desirability

Decision making is a planned process that results in the selection of a preferred course of action chosen from a number of variations and alternatives. The reality for many communities is that there are never enough resources available to do all of the things that people would like to do, and as a result, priorities must be established and compromises made.

When there are competing options, ideas, and projects, setting priorities and decision making can be both complex and contentious. Recreation master plans and facility feasibility studies, for example, can often have an extensive wish list of good ideas that all have varying degrees of merit and support. The wish list highlights all of the options that are desirable. The final priority list should identify the projects that are financially feasible. Sorting out which should be done first requires an absence of bias, good information, critical thinking, and sound judgement. The reality is that regardless of the decision taken, not everyone will agree.

It is helpful if there is a predesigned process that can assist in weighing options and establishing priorities based on appropriate criteria. Section 9.4 of this chapter presents a model that has been used to establish priorities when there are competing projects and interests that need to be weighed.

In the public sector, the objective in setting priorities and establishing the preferred option is to identify the course of action that provides the greatest benefit to the majority of people and represents the most efficient use of tax-supported resources. In the commercial and private sector, the decision is based on what the public is willing to pay in exchange for the services and facilities they receive.

Step 8. Action

The final step is to assemble the information and priorities into a written plan and begin the process of acting on the decisions and implementing the plan. As decisions, ideas, and projects are implemented, it is important to ensure that assumptions and factors used in developing the plan remain relevant and valid.

9.3 Priority Criteria Rating System—An Introduction

A priority criteria rating system is a structured method of determining the priority order of a number of competing options when developing a plan or having to make choices. The process is based on a form of logic that identifies the relative merit of one option versus another and is designed to minimize bias and special interest group pressure and influence.

The process takes into account multiple factors in setting priorities by first developing a wish list in consultation with stakeholders, defining the criteria against which each project or idea will be assessed, and then assigning a weight that each criterion represents in the process. This process can be applied to any decisions where there are a number of competing interests, alternatives, options, and ideas. For example, community grants programs for arts and recreation groups may receive hundreds of applications, and the priority criteria rating process allows decision makers to sort out the most worthy recipients based on predetermined criteria and an objective assessment of merit. The process can also be used to set priorities for new facilities in a long-range master plan or the desired components in a new recreation facility.

One such system, the PERC Priority Rating System was developed by Johnston (1976) and modified in subsequent priority ranking exercises in facility feasibility studies and parks and recreation master plans over the past thirty years.

Following is a summary of the process utilized in the Priority Rating System. A case study of the PERC Priority Rating System used in the City of Red Deer appears in Appendix C, and an example of the use of these principles applied to the site selection process appears in Appendix D.

9.4 The Priority Criterion Rating System—A Model for Decision Making

When attempting to establish the relative priority of a recommended action, it is important to utilize a bias-free system that ranks and weights each option based on predetermined criteria. The process of setting criteria, weighting, ranking, and rating ideas or options is best managed by involving a stakeholder steering committee in each step of the process. The more people involved in the process, the less likelihood of biased-based priority ranking as extreme views or bias are neutralized by having multiple participants in the process. The steps in the process are as follows:

Step 1. Facility Wish List

The first step is to develop a "wish list" of all potential ideas, components, or facility development projects. The list is typically compiled by conducting a demand analysis involving user group interviews, community survey, or other forms of public consultation.

Step 2. Establish Criteria

Once a wish list has been compiled, the next step is to define criteria by which each idea or option will be judged. The criteria must be developed locally in consultation with the community so that judgements are based on local community values, expectations, and circumstances. The criteria must also be consistent with and represent the goals and values the proponent of the project is seeking to achieve.

For example, when facility priorities are being considered in the public sector, the criteria might involve an assessment of how well a given facility serves the general public, including cost of use, cost of construction, extent of demand from a public survey, serves all ages versus limited age groups, seasonal versus year-round use, single-purpose components versus multipurpose use, etc.

Step 3. Rank Criteria

The next task is to rank order the criteria established to judge the merits of the proposed options. If there are ten criterion to be used to assess the facility options, they will be rank ordered from 1 (most important) to 10 (least important).

Step 4. Weight Criteria

Recognizing that each of the criteria may not be of equal importance, the relative merit of each criterion should then be weighted. This could mean that the criterion judged to be most important could be three times as important than the second criterion. The rank and weight are then applied to all facilities on the wish list to calculate their priority as suggested below.

Step 5. Priority Ranking

The final step is for the committee to evaluate each option or proposed facility on the wish list against each of the criteria and assign a priority based on an average of their scores using the following formula:

$$P = (C1 \times W1) + (C2 \times W2) + (C3 \times W3) + (C4 \times W4) + (C5 \times W5) + (C6 \times W6)$$
Key: (P=priority of facility, C=criteria and W=weight of criteria)

This process involves evaluating each facility type or facility component against each of the agreed-upon criteria. All members of the project committee score each facility individually, and then their scores are averaged to provide a numerical priority rating for all of the facilities under consideration. Figure 9.2 is a hypothetical model of the scoring system used in the evaluation. The study team first defines the criteria,

| Facility Type: Area | | | | |
Criteria	Sample of Criteria	Criteria Weight (W)	Unweighted Score 1-10	Total
1	Cost of Construction	2.0	4	8
2	Available Land	1.5	6	9
3	Serve Residents Equally	1.0	7	7
4	Open Year Round	1.0	9	9
Facility Score				33

Figure 9.2 Hypothetical Matrix Evaluation Model

and it is important to understand that they will be different for each planning exercise. Figure 9.2 lists just four examples.

A list of priorities will emerge based on which option has relatively more merit than other options. While the process has some limitations, it is a general reflection of the relative merits of competing wants, needs, and expectations. Appendices C and D illustrate how this process is implemented.

Section V
Types of Plans and Reports

10.0 Parks and Recreation Master Planning

10.1 Introduction

There are many types of plans that communities and organizations develop (Section 1.8, p. 13) based on the issues they need to resolve, the level of detail necessary, and the resources they have available. Each type of plan reflects a different level of planning in the overall planning hierarchy. In most communities, the General Plan is the framework document that establishes broad goals and policies that should guide and be consistent with all other community planning initiatives. Within community and leisure services organizations, there also is a hierarchy of planning that begins with the development of an integrated Parks and Recreation Master Plan from which other planning initiatives evolve. Each subsequent planning initiative provides a greater level of detail, clarity, and specifics (e.g., facility feasibility study, recreation program plan) related to issues, focus, cost, benefits, and implementation strategies.

10.2 Definition of a Parks and Recreation Master Plan

Parks and recreation master planning is defined as a broad-based, comprehensive process examining all of the factors and issues faced by a public sector parks and recreation services. A master plan is typically a forward-thinking, long-range document that provides a vision for the future (five years and beyond) and outlines the process and policies necessary to achieve that vision.

Until recently, most local governments organized their leisure services within an integrated stand-alone parks and recreation department, but today, many have adopted a community services model where parks and facilities might be located separately in public works or infrastructure departments, and recreation is managed within community services or community development. This means that in creating an integrated parks and recreation master plan, departments must cooperate and work together, but due to the dynamic relationship between facilities, parks, and programs, a plan that looks at these services together becomes that much more important.

In addition, the parks and recreation master plan must be consistent with the community's general or strategic plan and recognize the influence of the component parts of a general municipal plan. Industrial, commercial, and school location planning, transportation planning, and subdivision planning will all have an impact on the type and location of parks and recreation services needed.

A parks, recreation, and cultural master plan should reflect the overall vision for a liveable, vibrant, healthy, and exciting community by providing complementary facilities and events. It should build on the natural, cultural, social, and physical assets of the community, and the plan should provide a framework for strategic actions to enhance the parks, recreation, and cultural infrastructure thereby contributing to physical, social, and artistic opportunities and events. All stakeholders in the public and commercial and nonprofit sectors should be engaged in the process, and the general public should be consulted about their needs, interests, and expectations. The plan that results should provide the framework for decision making and the basis for a sound policy in the short- and long-term future.

10.3 Value of Master Planning

As the framework document for local government parks and recreation services, the master plan establishes the principles and rationale for decision making regarding the allocation of all human, physical, and fiscal resources. It establishes benchmarks and the basis for outcome assessment. The master plan should provide an opportunity for broad-based community consultation, clearly outline the role and responsibility of the public sector in recreation service provision, and encourage partnerships and strategic alliances.

In the absence of a master plan, there is a risk that decisions regarding service delivery and resource allocation will occur on an ad hoc basis.

10.4 Content of a Master Plan

The content is focused on general statements of principle and policies that guide decision making.

The master plan typically includes:

- Statement of vision, mission, and goals for parks and recreation services
- Operating policies, practices, and principles that guide service delivery
- Administration requirements and human resources, including the role and function of paid staff and volunteers
- Supply and demand for recreation programs and services
- Supply and demand for sport, recreation, and cultural facilities in the public, commercial, and not-for-profit sectors
- Financial analysis, including five-year operating and capital budgets
- Community partnerships and agreements
- Implementation strategies, including critical path (timelines) and resources needed to be successful
- Adoption and approval—Council bylaw

10.5 Master Planning Process

In order to make judgements about future recreation development, it is necessary to understand what services are now available, how use and demand for programs and facilities will change in the future, and what resources will be needed to support new initiatives and priorities that emerge from the planning process.

The first three sections of this book outlined the type of data that is needed to understand the community and develop plans for the future. Master planning relies heavily on the collection and analysis of all of these factors. It includes:

- A situational analysis of the internal and external operating environment
- A comprehensive demand analysis and assignment of priorities within the resources of the community to respond
- A means to implement, monitor, and evaluate progress

In its most basic form, the master planning process follows the same logical steps of other planning processes outlined herein, but the process is complex in that it must consider all aspects of the parks and recreation operation as well as the relationship and interaction with all other community services.

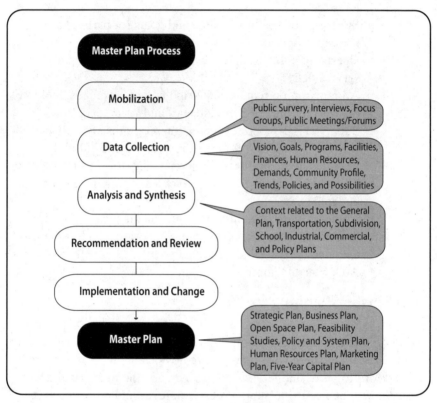

Figure 10.1 Master Planning Process

11.0 Facility Feasibility and Development

11.1 Introduction

When contemplating the construction of new recreation facilities, the consequences of error can be costly. Construction costs and land values have risen dramatically in recent years, and facility development decisions can be in the multimillion-dollar range. An error in judgement regarding the market for and long-term viability of a facility can have devastating consequences.

The facility development process involves a number of sequential steps that lead from vision to reality. Each step has equal importance in the process and provides checks and balances as it proceeds, allowing for informed decisions. The project can be halted at any stage in the process as more detailed information becomes available. The four key steps in the facility development process involve:

1. Planning and Feasibility
2. Design
3. Construction
4. Operations, Governance, and Management

The success of a facility depends on many factors. Sustainability and long-term viability depend on market demand and competition, location, capital costs, activity trends, quality of construction, image and

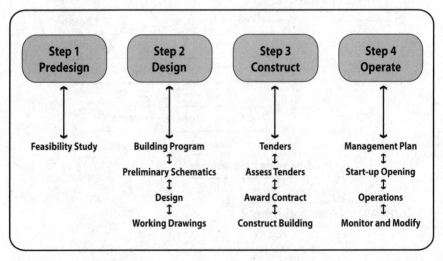

Figure 11.1 The Facility Development Process

appeal, operating policies, customer service, and the quality of the experience. If any one of these factors is not considered in the development process, success of the facility could be limited.

11.2 Pre-Design Planning and Feasibility Analysis

The first step in the process is to undertake a comprehensive feasibility study to determine the details and merit of the project. In some cases, this step is seen as less important than the steps to follow and viewed as

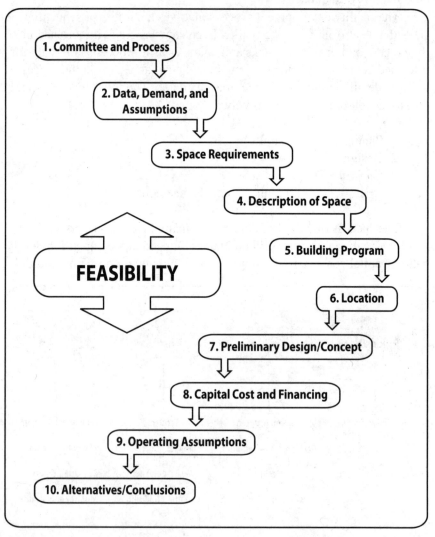

Figure 11.2 Feasibility Study Process

a time-consuming and unnecessary expense. However, when faced with multimillion-dollar decisions regarding facility development, the feasibility and long-term viability of the project may be the most important consideration.

The overall purpose of a feasibility study is to examine all related issues, consider alternative problem-solving strategies, and recommend the most cost-effective means to achieve the objective of the facility so that it is sustainable over the long term.

1. Committee and Process

Before undertaking a study, it is important to organize a study committee representative of the community's interests. Their role is to guide the process from start to finish, to clarify the goals for the project, and to agree on a decision-making process. The parameters of the feasibility study should then be defined and a decision made whether to do an in-house study or contract it out.

2. Data, Demand, and Assumptions

Decisions regarding the feasibility of a facility development will require data relevant to the facility type in question. Much like a master plan, it will need to consider the community profile, trends in activities related to the facility, current inventory of competing facilities, demand, and comparable standards for similar facilities.

Detail regarding the intended use and users of the space are critical to determining the scope, scale, quantity, and quality of the activity spaces to be included in the facility. For example, if an aquatic facility were not intended for competitive swim use, the size, shape, depth, and deck space would be very different from those of a competitive facility.

Attempting to plan a major facility that will be viable over the long term is extremely difficult. This requires a reasonably accurate prediction of future events, many of which may be out of the control of the planners. Assumptions must, therefore, be made about many of the issues to be resolved. The purpose of the study is to test these assumptions and either validate them or discount them. Predicting whether soccer will maintain its "market share" over the next ten years requires assumptions about the likelihood of future changes in demographics, leisure participation patterns, economic conditions, and social planning factors. Unfortunately, some assumptions can only be confirmed when the facility is operational.

This fact should prompt planners to develop facilities that are flexible and able to accommodate changing user patterns as they emerge.

3. Space Requirements

Data collected from potential users and user groups allow planners to define the appropriate quantity of space required to accommodate the activities that are planned. There are industry standards (Health/Fitness Facility Standards and Guidelines, 1997) that apply to various types of spaces, and they have been developed to ensure that adequate space is made available so that activities can be done in a safe and comfortable manner. For example, industry standards recommend 40–50 square feet per user in exercise areas. This allows planners to calculate the number of users a particular space can accommodate and how much space should be set aside for various activities and anticipated users.

4. Description of Space

The feasibility study should identify the design, layout, and quality of the space that is required. Qualitative standards related to floor cladding, lighting, ceiling height, circulation space, air quality, and ventilation vary with the type of program and the intended use of the space. Again, there are recommended standards for activity spaces, but they vary greatly based on the level of play, quality of the experience, and expectations of the users. As an example, storage areas do not need the same level of standard as public use areas, and architects need to know how space will be used so that they can provide the quality of finishes and furnishing necessary to complement intended use.

5. Building Program

The building program of requirements is a summary of all spaces including programmed activity space, as well as space set aside for circulation, mechanical, storage, reception, washrooms, and other public areas. This analysis provides information about the magnitude of space required for various functions and the capacity that each space has available for use. Figure 11.3 illustrates the preliminary building program for the Bronx Park/Good Neighbours Centre (Harper, 2006).

AREA	COMPONENT	SPACE IN SQ. FT.	CAPACITY
1. The Meeting Zone	Main Assembly/Activation Hall	4,000	350
2. Wellness Zone	General Activity Room	2,000	35
	Dance/Fitness Studio	1,500	25
	Resistance Training Area	2,000	75
	Wellness Case Rooms 3x80	240	6
	Dressing Rooms 4x300	1,200	25
	Locker/Shower 2x500	1,000	80
3. Social Zone	Games Room	1,500	40
	Community Lounge	800	60
	Kitchen/Canteen/Coffee	1,000	N/A
4. Culture and Education Zone	Computer Lab	1,000	20
	Multi-Media Centre	2,000	100
	Creative Arts Studio	1,000	20
	Home Improvement Shop	1,500	15
5. Administration Zone	Foyer/Reception	1,000	40
	Board Room	500	12
	Offices–6	720	6
	Storage/Copy Room	800	
SUB TOTAL		24,260	
6. Unprogrammed/Support	Janitor	175	
	Mechanical/Equipment Storage	1,600	
	Men's WC	300	
	Women's WC	525	
	Storage	700	
7. Circulation Space		7,740	
TOTAL		35,300	

Figure 11.3 Summary of Building Plan and Indoor Space Requirements

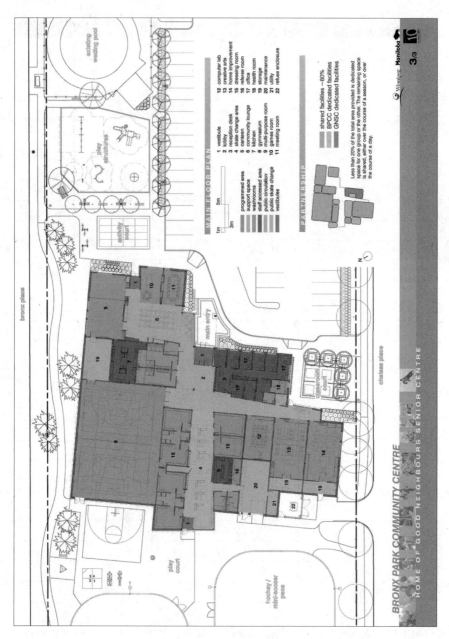

Figure 11.4 Bronx Park/Good Neighbours Centre Schematic

Capital Cost Implications

Indoor Space:

1. Bronx Park Good Neighbours Centre (35,300 ft2 @ $100-$140 ft2)	$3,500,000
2. Fees @ 10%	$350,000
3. Equipment Allowance	$200,000
4. Contingencies	$100,000
5. Finances and Administration @ 2%	$70, 000
6. Site Development (includes parking)	$150,000
Total (Indoor) Development Costs	$4,370,000

Source: J. Harper/Number Ten Architects

Table # 11.5 Cost of Bronx Park/Good Neighbours Centre
(Source: J. Harper, Number TEN Architectual Group, Winnipeg, Manitoba)

6. Location

Choosing the location for a proposed facility is an important but complex issue. Location is one of the most critical factors related to facility visibility, accessibility, and viability. Factors such as land values, site servicing costs, zoning, public transportation, environmental regulations, and neighborhood compatibility all affect decisions regarding location.

A case study related to the matrix assessment approach to facility site selection (Harper & Searle, 1990) can be found in Appendix D. The model identifies all of the factors to be considered and rates and ranks multiple site options against predetermined criteria to assist in making an objective decision on facility location.

7. Preliminary Conceptual Design

Once the building program and qualitative standards have been developed, a preliminary schematic or bubble diagram can be developed. This level of design is used to illustrate special relationships, circulation space between components, magnitude of each component, location on the property, and site compatibility.

8. Capital Cost and Financing

A reliable capital cost estimate for the proposed facility at this stage is premature because there are so many unknowns that could affect the final cost dramatically. There are several ways to predict the end cost of the construction of a facility. The most accurate method is to cost out all components of the facility once working drawings and detailed design are completed. At the conceptual facility planning stage, more planners would estimate a "cost of magnitude" or unit cost of construction based on the square footage of the building and the going-rate cost of comparable buildings. The real capital cost of the building won't be known until working drawings are complete and tenders are received from qualified contractors.

In addition to the actual building, other cost factors that need to be taken into consideration include the cost of design, legal work, permits, financing, site development, and site servicing. Once these are added, the end cost of the facility can be greatly increased. Table 11.5 (Harper, 2006) illustrates the impact of ancillary costs on the final building cost.

This financial information, while preliminary in nature, gives the building proponent an estimate of the magnitude of the costs involved in development.

9. Operating Assumptions

The long-term viability of a facility depends on the relationship between operating costs and projected sources of revenue. In a commercial facility, where the motive for development is profit, evidence of sufficient demand is needed to warrant the financial risks associated with the facility operation. In addition to recovering the direct costs of the facility operation, commercial operators also must recover interest on loans or mortgages against the building and allow for a return of profit to the owners and investors.

Community arenas and pools have typically been developed by the public sector because of the high costs of operation and the limited opportunity to generate sufficient revenue to be profitable. The average going rate price for ice rental is between $75 and $150 per hour (youth vs. adult) and operating costs can range between $200 and $300 per hour. In the public sector, most major facilities are subsidized so that they are affordable. Each municipality decides what level of subsidy can be justified based on how much they believe all taxpayers should contribute to provide the facility and how much users should pay to access the facility.

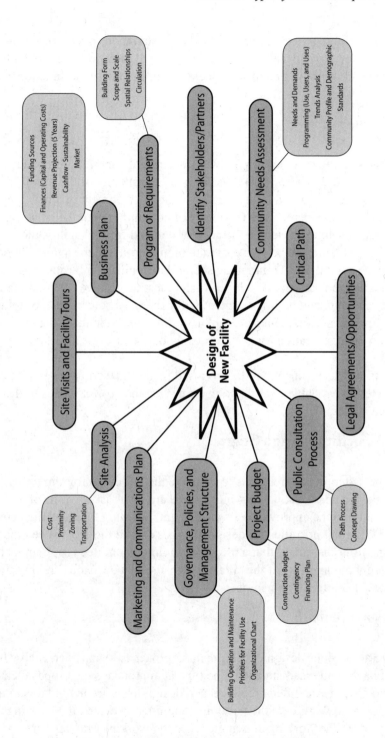

Figure 11.6 Predesign Facility Planning Process

A preliminary cost estimate based on assumptions of cost of operation, market demand, and willingness to pay will provide an understanding of the level of return or subsidy necessary for the facility to function economically.

10. Conclusions

At this stage, the relationship between desirability and feasibility is examined. Figure 11.6 (p. 107) illustrates the complexity of the feasibility study process where all issues related to the development of a new facility must be considered. The feasibility of continuing with the planning process is weighed based on the need or demand for the facility, the likelihood that it will be viable over the long term, and the availability of adequate capital. In a commercial sector development, a business case or business plan is usually developed to demonstrate to investors that the facility is viable, and their investment will generate a suitable rate of return. In the public sector, the business plan outlines the benefits of the facility and the justification for public subsidy on the basis of a cost/benefit analysis.

If it is determined that the proposed facility is warranted, and it is expected to be viable over the long term, then the project moves to the design stage.

11.3 Facility Design Stage

The next step in the process is to translate the building program into a final design and working drawings. There are many issues to resolve leading up to the approval of a final design, including more detailed costing and setting priorities for design changes should the cost exceed the budget. It is customary that a project planning committee is appointed to represent the interests of the client and ensure that decisions are made in a timely and objective fashion.

Design Approach

There are various design/development approaches to consider, each with advantages and disadvantages. The typical approach is the proposal call method, where qualified architects and design firms are invited to submit a proposal to work with the building committee to design the building and prepare the working drawings. Once the working drawings are approved and a cost estimate agreed upon, then building contractors are invited to bid on the construction of the facility, and the architect over-sees the construction. In recent years, building construction costs have increased dramatically as the cost of materials has increased and the availability of skilled labor has declined. These factors have created un-certainty in facility planning, design, and development.

Another approach is called the design-build method, where the de-sign team and contractor work together to produce a design and cost for the client based on the approved budget. The theory is that this approach is better suited to controlling costs as the building is designed. If this ap-proach is chosen, it is useful to assign a project manager to the develop-ment. The project manager works on behalf of the planning committee or client to ensure that costs are controlled, construction proceeds on sched-ule, and disputes are resolved as they arise.

Cost and Design

During the design development phase, preliminary schematics are drawn up, and the design process becomes more and more refined. In effect, the concept plan is translated into working drawings and more detailed cost estimates are prepared. A rendering (figure 11.7.a) of the planned facil-ity is usually done at this stage so that the image and visual impact of the design can be interpreted to the client and the community. Figure 11.7b illustrates the evolution of the design process exploring various color op-tions. While the final look of a facility (figure 11.7.c) can vary from the preliminary concept once client feedback has been received, the objective is to build the final product as close to the original concept as possible.

As more detailed costs are developed, the project manager and plan-ning committee must make decisions related to their priorities for the facility and areas where they can compromise on space and quality. In the facility design process, there are several variables that affect the end cost of the facility. These include the number of components or spaces in the com-plex, the size of each space, and the quality of finishes and furnishing.

In a multipurpose facility development, there may be a number of components such as a pool, arena, fitness studio, gym, meeting rooms, and storage facilities. If the preliminary cost estimates of the facility are too high, then one option is to prioritize the components and develop the facility in several phases as funding becomes available. A second option is to downsize each of the components or selected components to meet the budget, and a third option is to compromise on the quality of the fur-nishings, finishes, and fixtures planned for the building. This can include everything from floor coverings to lighting fixtures and, depending on the

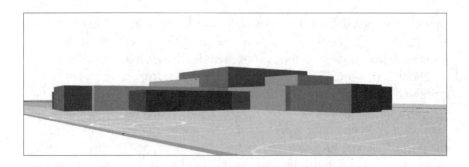

Figure 11.7a Preliminary Schematic Block Massing

Figure 11.7b An Intermediate Development Rendering Exploring Different Materials

Figure 11.7c Final Rendering—As Built

(Figures 11.7a—c Courtesy of Doug Hanna, Number TEN Architectural Group, Winnipeg, Manitoba)

quality of the product needed, can generate significant savings without compromising the function of the building.

Once these decisions have been made, the final design and working drawings can be approved and the project moved to the construction phase.

11.4 Facility Construction Stage

If the building was planned using the proposal call approach, then the next step is to prepare tender documents and conduct a call for tenders from qualified contractors. Tenders are used to ensure that each contractor is bidding on exactly the same thing within a given time frame, and the bids can be easily compared.

The reason for the tender call is to invite competitive bids to construct the building, but the lowest bidder may not necessarily be the best choice for the project. The planning committee and architect also consider the experience and track record of the contractors and their capacity to construct the building on time, on specification, and within budget.

If the design-build method has been chosen, then the project manager and building committee work closely with the contractor so that the building conforms to the specifications set out at the cost budgeted for the project.

11.5 Operation, Governance, and Maintenance

Once the building is completed, there will be a final inspection of the construction and any deficiencies itemized and remedied. There is usually a building warranty period during which time the client can request that deficiencies that appear be remedied. During this period, it will be important to keep meticulous records and monitor and report all deficiencies as they are detected.

Every facility needs a start-up period where the operating systems are checked out to ensure they function as they were designed. The management and facility operation staff will take some time to get all of the systems operating as they were designed and familiarize themselves with unique aspects of the facility operating systems. Once the building is operating, it is useful to develop a strategic plan and/or business plan that will contemplate all of the issues likely to arise and develop the strategies necessary to deal with them. This includes strategies around program design, marketing, user policies (rates and fees), maintenance management, and budget and finance.

12.0 Strategic Planning

12.1 Introduction

Strategic planning is an essential tool for organizational management and development. Balmer (1988) defined strategic planning as "a process through which an organization envisions its future and develops the necessary procedures and operation to achieve that future. It is goal directed and issue based. It clarifies the business of an organization and responds to key current issues affecting the organization's ability to deliver and remain relevant."

Everyone involved in the process should recognize that change is inevitable, quantitative information is essential, and both political and economic realities must be recognized and incorporated into the plan that results.

Strategic planning is one part of the process leading to organizational change. The other component of the process is strategic management, and there is a dynamic relationship between strategic planning and strategic management. It lies in the realization that the success of strategic planning is not based on the ideas and plans that are developed but in the outcomes and organizational change that occur.

12.2 Benefits of Strategic Planning

There are many benefits associated with strategic planning and it is an exercise that every organization should conduct on a regular basis. The top ten benefits include:

- Creates an environment for organizational change and renewal
- Develops buy-in on the part of people involved in the organization
- Builds on strengths
- Establishes clear direction
- Identifies barriers to success
- Fixes problems
- Focuses on priorities

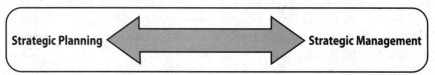

Figure 12.1 Dynamic Interaction-Planning and Management

- Promotes team building through consensus
- Commits everyone to a plan of action
- Provides a basis for evaluation and measurable outcome assessment

12.3 Process for Strategic Planning

There are several models in use to guide the process of strategic planning, but perhaps the most common is the issue- or goal-based approach outlined in Figure 12.2.

Vision and Mission

Assuming that the process is being conducted with a well-established organization, the first step is to revisit the vision, mission, and goals of the organization so that everyone begins the process with a common understanding of what the organization seeks to achieve. At the end of the process, it is useful to revisit the mission statement again to ensure that it continues to reflect the central direction of the organization following the planning exercise.

Environmental or Situational Analysis

The environmental analysis involves a review of both the internal and external operating environment of the organization. Examining the external environment could involve a survey of consumers to gauge expectations, a community scan to identify trends and changes with respect to the target market for services, or focus groups that react to the services of the organization.

A facilitated S.W.O.T. process in a workshop setting takes place with all of the stakeholders of the organization involved. The strengths, weaknesses, opportunities, and threats are all identified and form the basis for the problem-solving component of the process that follows. The internal scan of the organization might also include an organizational audit or organizational health assessment involving the key personnel in the organization. This process assists in identifying some of the weaknesses that might exist and is focused on fact-based information.

Think Creatively / Plan Strategically

An analysis of the issues is undertaken and creative ideas to build on strengths and deal with weaknesses are developed. Each strategy is fully explored, and detailed action or implementation plans are created that

specify the implications of action in terms of time, resources, and anticipated outcomes or benefits. Each of these strategies is then prioritized
based on economic realities and outcome measures are defined.

Manage Strategically / Evaluate Systematically

An important component of the strategic plan is the process developed to
review, monitor, and evaluate progress. The strategic development plan
is done in sufficient detail so that it can be used as an ongoing tool to
measure progress and each employee's contribution to the organization.
It should be included as a regular agenda item at all staff meetings, and
there should be a detailed review every six months to ensure that targets
are being met and that the assumptions on which the plan was based are
still valid.

The most important aspect of evaluation is to be sure that the right
things are being measured. Following the development of the plan, the
focus is on strategically managing the strategies that were developed.
Most managers now recognize that the important outcomes of an organization are not the number of programs that are created or the amount of
money that is spent, but rather the benefits that result from the creation of
programs and the impact they have had on the users and the community
that is being served. Outcome assessment now relies on the design of appropriate performance indicators.

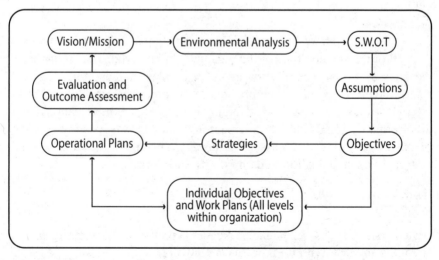

Figure 12.2 The Strategic Planning Process

13.0 Business Planning

13.1 Introduction to Business Planning

In many respects, a business plan is an extension of the strategic planning process in that it requires clear goals and an understanding of the internal and external operating environment. Unlike strategic planning where the focus is on management and organizational development, business planning focuses on the long-term viability of a program, product, service, or facility and is intended to build a convincing business case.

A business plan is a written document that outlines in detail the concept of the business, the primary objectives, core services, target market, skills and experience of personnel involved in the enterprise, and the resources needed to achieve its targets. This information is necessary to illustrate why the business is likely to be successful.

13.2 Components of a Business Plan

The components of a business plan (Figure 13.1) include several of the steps used to develop a strategic plan. It is important to articulate the vision of the business and the primary objectives that will drive the initiative. Conducting a situational analysis will identify the strengths, weaknesses, opportunities, and threats that might affect the success of the business, and strategies should be developed and prioritized to serve as a guide. In addition to these components, a business plan is unique in that it includes details of market strategies and financial projections that illustrate its viability and profitability.

A. Organization Concept and Business Profile

In addition to a description of the vision, goals, and objectives of the business, this section of a business plan should include a history and description of the business or project and information about its success or potential for success in the marketplace. It should also include information about the background and experience of the project proponents and management team.

B. Situational Analysis

Similar to the organizational health assessment and S.W.O.T. analysis done in a strategic planning process, a business plan should also address

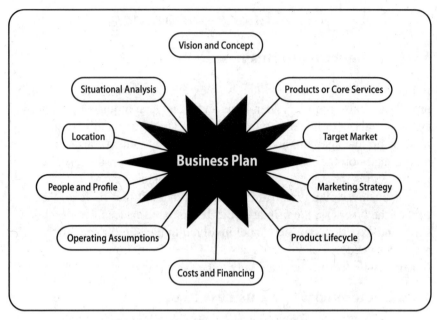

Figure 13.1 Business Planning Factors

these issues. In addition, information related to industry trends, health of the business sector, standards, and assumptions regarding its place in the business community all assist in building the rationale for the business and the plan that follows.

C. Core Services—Product Focus

This section includes a detailed description of the core service or product being promoted and its place in the current market. An analysis of the unique attributes of the business or product and the competition it is likely to encounter in the marketplace should form part of the plan.

D. Product Life Cycle and Market Strategies

It is important to include information related to the expected product life cycle and the steps that will need to be taken to maintain its relevance in the market place and be sustainable over the long term. Any facility, product, or service will go through a life cycle where interest in the product and consumption will change over time. The speed at which products move through the life cycle is affected by many factors, all of which planners must be aware and monitor regularly.

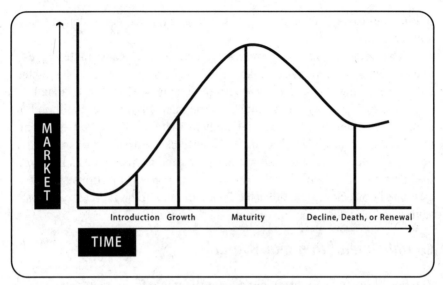

Figure 13.2 Product Lifecycle
Source: Edginton & Griffith, 1983

The most important issue relates to how an organization or business will react as the use and popularity of a product changes. Maintaining "market share" is based on a solid understanding of how price, place, and product fit within the marketplace as well as detailed knowledge about the target market, customer profile, going rate pricing, effective marketing, and communication strategies.

E. Operations

A description of the proposed approach to operations should include information about the governance model in place or proposed to manage the enterprise as well as methods of operation, inventory and financial controls, availability of human resources (labor force), and operating schedule on a seasonal and daily basis. Some of these factors will be based on assumptions until such time as the business is operational and more is known about the operating climate.

F. Financial Plan

The financial plan forms the most important element of a business plan because it translates the data and factors outlined in the conceptual plan into a cost analysis of the feasibility and viability of the business. This analysis is based on a number of assumptions about the marketplace, willingness to pay, sustainability of the product, price point, demand, and consumption.

The financial analysis provides projections of the anticipated revenue and expenses required to operate the business as well as costs related to debt servicing. The projected operating results spell out in financial terms the rationale for proceeding with the business and the likelihood of success. An example of a financial analysis that was developed as a commercial tourist attraction (Figure 13.3) outlines the assumptions related to attendance, fees, and staff requirements, and the projected costs involved in running such a facility. If the revenue or expense projections are not estimated correctly, then either the fees will need to be increased or cost savings achieved so that the operation is sustainable.

G. Implementation and Evaluation

The business plan should set out a clear timetable for implementation with timelines and benchmarks developed in a critical path format. To assure all stakeholders that the business will be managed effectively and that their investment will be managed carefully, it will be important to illustrate how outcomes will be measured and performance evaluated.

There are many excellent guides to business planning available, but the Canadian Business Service Centre operated by the Canada and Manitoba Governments has an excellent interactive web site (www.cbsc.org/ibp) that has a self-administered template to assist interested parties in preparing a business plan. It remains on the site and can be modified and updated as circumstances change and new information becomes available.

Projected Operating Results

	1995 (1/2 Year)	1996	1997	1998	1999	2000
Key Statistics						
Total Attendance	425,000	850,000	800,000	750,000	750,000	750,000
Paid Attendance	382,500	765,000	720,000	675,000	675,000	675,000
Average Ticket Price	$6.75	$6.75	$7.65	$7.65	$8.55	$8.55
Full-Time Equivalent Employees	66	66	66	66	66	66
Revenue/Income						
Admissions	$2,868,750	$5,737,500	$6,120,000	$5,737,500	$6,412,500	$6,412,500
Merchandise	191,000	397,280	430,477	465,694	503,039	523,161
Concessions	127,500	265,200	259,584	253,094	263,218	273,747
Special Events	72,000	180,000	324,000	432,000	432,000	432,000
Memberships	125,000	520,000	594,880	618,675	701,915	701,915
Total	3,384,250	7,099,980	7,728,941	7,506,963	8,312,672	8,343,323
Expenses						
Payroll Related	1,384,819	2,880,426	2,995,643	3,115,469	3,240,089	3,369,691
General & Administrative	221,000	459,680	478,067	497,189	517,077	537,761
Exhibit Maintenance	0	200,000	208,000	216,320	224,973	233,972
Utilities	127,918	266,070	276,712	287,781	299,292	311,264
Land Lease	100,000	200,000	200,000	200,202	200,202	200,202
Building Maintenance	75,000	156,000	162,240	168,730	175,479	182,498
Contract Services	126,200	262,496	272,996	283,916	295,273	307,084
Other Operating	15,000	31,200	32,448	33,746	35,096	36,500
Marketing & Promotion	675,000	702,000	631,800	568,620	591,365	615,021
Total	2,724,937	5,157,872	5,257,906	5,371,973	5,578,846	5,793,993
Operating Income (Loss) Before Capital Expenses	$659,313	$1,942,108	$2,471,035	$2,134,990	$2,733,826	$2,549,330
Exhibit Refurbishment	0	520,000	757,120	562,432	818,901	1,094,988
Capital Reserve	162,500	325,000	325,000	325,000	325,000	325,000
Operating Cash Flow	$496,813	$1,097,108	$1,388,915	$1,247,558	$1,589,925	$1,129,342

Figure 13.3 Sample Financial Plan

14.0 Open Space Planning—A Systems Approach

14.1 Introduction

Parks and open spaces are critical components in developing healthy, holistic communities and contribute greatly to the quality of the urban environment. Open space in urban centers must be designated by policy and strategically planned to meet the needs of the community and provide the many benefits that result from the availability of open space.

Due to the great variety of land and open space available and the many types of uses that are possible, a systems approach to planning is necessary. In general terms, systems planning is a predesign process used to outline goals, standards, and space required to meet the direct and indirect needs of the users. In addition, the process organizes space by type of use, classification, and component so that the distribution and location of park and open space is done in an equitable and systematic way throughout the community.

This section provides an overview of the systems approach to open space planning and illustrates the principles involved in the process as well as the six-step approach to defining, categorizing, and developing a comprehensive parks and open space system in a community.

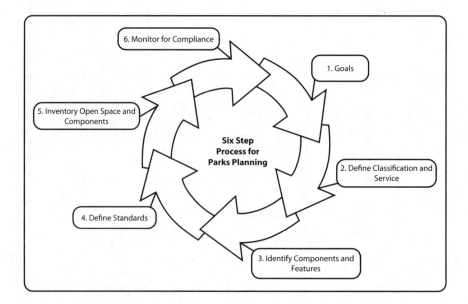

Figure 14.1 Process for the Systems Approach to Park Development

14.2 Benefits of Parks and Open Space

Parks are often referred to as the "lungs of the city," and they represent essential components of a healthy community. Parks and open space provide environmental protection and preservation, visual and aesthetic appeal, places for physical, social, and spiritual activity, and are economic generators for communities and their residents. Parks provide buffers between residential and industrial development, linear linkages and transportation corridors, increase property values, and are a factor in decisions about business relocation. Parks also serve as water retention resources, provide shade that affects temperature and climate, offer habitat for wildlife, and help to shape the image of the community.

14.3 Definition of Open Space

Open space has been defined in many ways, but in a landmark document in park development, Jack Wright (1976) provided an inclusive definition that highlights the type, purpose, and benefits of open space:

> "All urban land and water, both publicly and privately owned, that is open to the sky and reasonably accessible to freely chosen activity or visual exploration, and that serves people and nature in an educative, aesthetic, productive, protective, or recreative way."

This definition describes a total open space system within which individual components have both visual and practical value, contributing equally to the goals and objectives of the parks and recreation system.

14.4 Six-Step Approach to Open Space Planning

The open space planning process involves a sequence of steps that begins with establishing goals to guide the system, an assessment of available parks and open space resources, a definition of park categories and components, a description of qualitative and quantitative standards, service gaps or deficiencies in the system, and strategies to maintain and improve the current supply in relation to community expectations and standards. Following is a complete description of each of the steps in the process.

GOALS–Parks and Open Space

To preserve and protect open space for the enjoyment of present and future generations thereby ensuring an aesthetically pleasing environment and adequate space for outdoor leisure experiences.

OBJECTIVES:

1. Provision of Open Space
To guarantee the availability, location and adequate supply of parks and open space by developing appropriate long-range planning and land acquisition policies.

2. Preservation, Development and Conservation
To ensure the protection and development of natural aesthetic features and the provision of public access to such features in an effort to contribute to a greater understanding and appreciation of the environment.

3. Beautify the Community
To develop programs that enhance and beautify the community. The extent to which its residents see a community as being visually pleasing directly relates to the potential for creating community identity, spirit and pride.

4. Interpret the Environment
To create opportunities for every local resident to learn about, understand, relate to and experience all aspects of his/her environment.

5. Reflection and Escape
To develop spaces in the community parks system that allow for escape, reflection, contact with nature and relaxation in a natural environment.

6. Maintenance of Open Space
To ensure that open space is systematically maintained in order to enhance the environment and provide functional, safe and appealing parks and outdoor areas.

Figure 14.2 Goals and Objectives for the Parks System

Step 1. Goals for Parks and Open Space

Goals for the parks and open space system should be written to reflect the organization's responsibility for environmental stewardship, qualitative and quantitative development standards, approach to maintenance, policies governing use, and long-term sustainability of the resource. As an example, the following goals and objectives were adopted to guide the development of the parks system in one rural Manitoba community (Winkler, 2000).

Step 2. Parks and Open Space Classification System

Typically, open space is classified on the basis of the quantity and quality of the space. It is also important to take into account the end use of the space in any classification system. Both active and passive uses must be considered and planned so that they don't conflict with one another.

Communities of various sizes will modify the park classification to suit their geographic and population size. In large cities the classification system may be expanded and subdivided into smaller, more representative descriptions (sub-precinct, neighborhood, community, district, and region) of the space and people to be served. For small- to medium-sized communities, the following classification system would be suitable to guide the acquisition and development of park and open space now and in the future. This system describes both the level of park development and the type of parks that fit within the category. All spaces in the community should fit within these categories.

Level I—Neighborhood Level

Neighborhood open space serves a small user radius and is designed to provide facilities in close proximity to the user with a more localized point of identity. Neighborhoods are defined by a combination of factors, including physical or geographic boundaries, political boundaries, social or cultural boundaries, or other natural or physical features that separate one neighborhood from another. Neighborhood open space generally serves a population of approximately 2,000 residents and would, therefore, serve the same population and user radius as an elementary school. The majority of users should not have to cross a major thoroughfare to reach the area, and park space should be located to serve a user radius of approximately 400 meters. Typical of every standard, great variance can occur depending upon local conditions such as the presence of major thoroughfares, rivers, and other natural boundaries that separate residential areas from each other.

Type A. Characteristics of Tot Lots and Playgrounds

For the most part, tot lots and playgrounds are developed as a component of a larger neighborhood or school site. This approach is highly desirable and should be encouraged as it represents the

Level I Neighborhood Level	
Type:	a. Tot Lot / Playground
	b. Neighborhood Park
Level II Community Level	
Type:	a. Athletic Park
	b. Natural / Passive Park
Level III Regional Level	
Type:	a. Athletic Park
	b. Natural / Passive Park
	c. Special Use areas

Table 14.1 Parks Classification System

most efficient use of park space. Stand-alone tot lots are single-purpose components of the open space system and are expensive to develop and maintain and often underutilized in relation to other types of multiuse open space. In many cases, the tot lot provides a substitute for backyard play areas and therefore may be better utilized if located adjacent to high-density developments such as apartment complexes. As an example, Map #1 illustrates playground locations, service radius, and proximity to residents in the Town of Winkler. This illustration can also be used to locate neighborhoods that might be underserved by neighborhood tot lots and playgrounds.

There are distinct advantages to developing larger playground sites with a greater variety and quality of components that better serve the community.

There may be unique circumstances where it is necessary to develop a stand-alone playground or tot lot. This level of development should only occur when larger pieces of property cannot be easily assembled, in locations adjacent to high-density, high-rise apartments, or where the neighborhood is without an adequate supply of land.

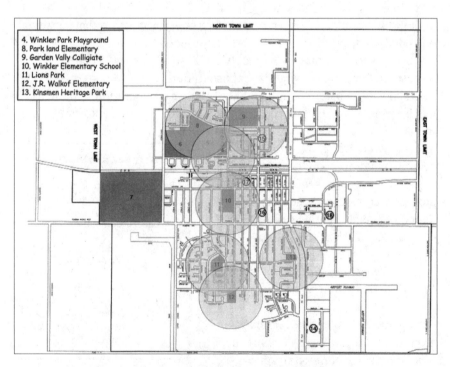

4. Winkler Park Playground
8. Park land Elementary
9. Garden Vally Colligiate
10. Winkler Elementary School
11. Lions Park
12. J.R. Walkof Elementary
13. Kinsmen Heritage Park

**Map #1- Playground Location and Service Radius,
Town of Winkler—Program Service Area**

Type B. Characteristics of Neighborhood Parks

Wherever possible, a neighborhood park should be a minimum of five acres, located adjacent to, and including, elementary school grounds. This allows for joint development of the community/school site and encourages flexible use of available space. Neighborhood park sites provide both active and passive recreation opportunities. Included in the site should be a children's playground area, passive recreation/observation area for adults, and playfields for children up to fifteen years of age. It should include athletic fields, creative playground equipment, parents' observation areas, buffering and landscaping, tree planting, and park benches. It could also include toboggan hills, park benches, and hard surface areas for court games. In some cases, neighborhood parks include spray pads and skateboard areas.

In order that this size of play space is made available, it might be necessary to dispose of smaller parcels of existing land, or only accept park reserve in new subdivisions that meet the desired standard previously outlined.

Level II—Community Level

In general, community level open space is designed to serve two or three neighborhoods. It is made up of larger tracts of open space where outdoor facilities can be developed to a higher standard than that available on a neighborhood level and would be impractical to develop to this standard in every neighborhood. It typically serves the population within a middle school/ high school service radius and provides higher quality, more diversity, and broader choice of amenities.

Type A. Characteristics of Community Athletic Parks

It is desirable to consolidate major outdoor recreation activities into one space where land is available. Doing so provides a multipurpose area that is more economical to maintain and more dynamic in its development. Economies can be achieved because multiple activities can be served by central support buildings, parking lots, change room facilities, and concession areas.

Such a site provides a higher standard of maintenance and development and caters to more senior level games, local tournaments, exhibitions, clinics, and events. Areas for softball, baseball, soccer, football, track and field, tennis courts, and special events should be developed on such a site. Other amenities that could be developed in conjunction with athletic parks could include a skateboard area, spray pool or water park, outdoor pool, beach volleyball, and hard surface games areas.

The athletic park should be centrally located and provide adequate parking, spectator areas, water fountains, and washrooms. The minimum size for such a facility should be 15 acres.

Type B. Characteristics of Community Passive / Natural Parks

The natural park is best distinguished from an athletic or active park in that it is nonprogrammed and provides for informal, passive recreation. Generally, a natural or passive park would have minimal development, although certain areas could be developed for more intensive recreation use than others. Generally, heavily-treed buffer areas characterize these larger expanses of open space and could be developed adjacent to a tot lot or children's play area to serve as an observation area for parents. But it should be well-buffered to maintain opportunities for passive recreation, contemplation, and relaxation. In Winnipeg, Central Park and Kings Park are two examples of passive parks areas.

Level III—Regional Level

Regional level space is set aside to serve the needs of the entire community and typically provides one-of-a-kind areas and facilities that would be impractical to provide at the neighborhood or community level. These serve as a focus for both passive and active recreation and are often used to attract tourists, special events, and participants from beyond the community.

Type A. Regional Athletic Park

A regional athletic park typically is a large-scale, multipurpose outdoor athletic complex that houses high-quality facilities to serve the competitive needs of senior level play in a Class I setting. Fields, pitches, and diamonds built in a regional athletic park would have bleacher seating, lighted fields, outfield fencing, dugouts, concessions, scoreboard, change rooms with showers, and perimeter site fencing for control.

These athletic parks are designed to attract high-level play, tournaments, clinics, and special events. They can serve as tourist attractions and host major events and, therefore, it may be desirable that they conform to the standards established by sport-governing bodies so that they could also qualify to host competitive play at the provincial, national, and international levels.

Examples of these types of facilities in Winnipeg would include the John Bloomberg Athletic Complex, the Canad Inns Stadium, and the MTS Centre.

Type B. Regional Natural/Passive Park

Regional level natural parks are special areas in many communities featuring ornamental flower gardens, hiking trails, water features, and quiet areas. The natural park could have areas for day use such as reading, relaxing, picnicking, jogging, cycling, hiking, and water-related facilities.

It is important to protect and preserve any natural or unique features and at the same time, provide access to features of particular environmental significance or natural beauty. In Winnipeg, Assiniboine, St. Vital, and East Kildonan Park all fit the definition of a regional level natural park.

Type C. Regional Special Use Parks and Areas

Speciality use parks could include a wide variety of components such as landscaped areas, linear pathways, trails and buffers, natural interpretative areas, and single-purpose areas and facilities. Following is a definition of each type of special use park area.

Type C.1 Definition of Landscaped Areas

A landscaped area is carefully designed and extensively developed to provide a pleasing visual impact. Only passive park activities (e.g., sun tanning, reading, socializing, walking) would be encouraged within such an area. The primary purpose would be to improve the image or aesthetic appearance of an area or to establish a buffer to provide relief from urban, industrial, and commercial development. Such areas are meant to provide visual focal points for the community.

Often, such spaces are developed in conjunction with major civic buildings that are meant to reflect the "image" of a community and create a positive impression. They are also usually part of a major park area where tourists, town center employees, and resident shoppers may stop and relax. Other locations for landscaped areas are at the major entrances to the community to create an initial positive impression and are sometimes called image routes.

These can be high maintenance spaces with correspondingly high maintenance costs, but encouraging voluntary initiative can assist in developing and maintaining such spaces. The national Communities in Bloom program recognize the importance of these types of spaces to communities and annually recognize communities that have excelled in their development.

Type C.2 Definition of Linear Pathways, Trails, and Buffers

It is desirable to establish a network of pathways and linkages between park spaces that provide access, continuity, and complete the open space network. Individual sites, once linked, provide for a greater variety of use and safer access. Linear parks also create the impression that there is more space than actually exists by providing depth to the system. Linear pathways and linkages (See Map #2) are important in themselves in that they provide trails for hiking, jogging, cycling, cross-country skiing, and walking, and as such, form an important part of the transportation system in the community.

Type C.3 Definition of Natural Interpretative Areas

The human and natural history in a community provides an opportunity to develop unique park spaces. Areas of significant historical value should be identified and preserved so that present and future generations can enjoy and learn from them. Environmental preserve and natural interpretative areas such as the Living Prairie Museum, Assiniboine Forrest, Oak Hammock Marsh, and Fort Whyte Interpretive Centre are examples of this.

Type C.4 Single Purpose Specialty Use Areas

Special use areas and facilities are typically "one of a kind" facilities or spaces that provide unique recreation opportunities. Typically they have been developed to a high degree for a single purpose or exclusive use. Examples of speciality use areas are:

- Golf Course
- Outdoor Stage
- Shooting Range
- Conservatory
- Campground

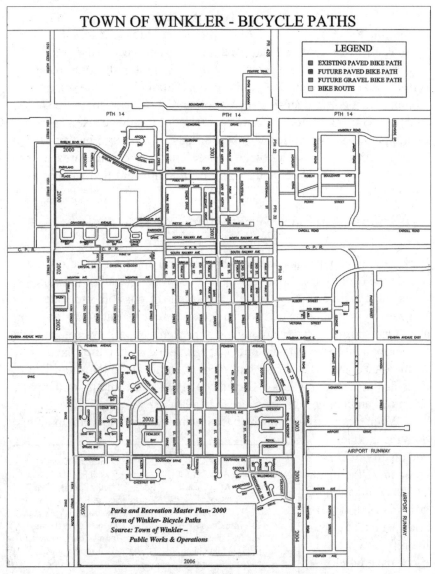

Map #2 - Town of Winkler—Bicycle Paths

- Mini-golf
- Agricultural Society Grounds
- Skateboard Park
- Equestrian Riding Ring
- Museums and Heritage Parks

Because of the diversity and type of special use areas, it is almost impossible to adopt any standard for provision of these spaces. Decisions about each space must be made on a project-by-project basis.

Special use areas are often very limited in their ability to meet service objectives related to public good. Although they are important elements in a comprehensive recreation and parks system, these spaces often serve special interest group requirements, and because of this, municipal tax subsidization will be limited or difficult to justify. Hence, responsibility for construction and operation of special use areas often rests primarily with specific user groups, a nonprofit organization, or the commercial sector.

Step 3. Open Space Components and Features

Each park and open space area has both natural and man-made features that define it as a park. Not every park space will have all of the components listed below, but they make up the range of possible site features and activity components that people seek when they visit a park or open area. One approach to developing a comprehensive park system is to vary the components, size, and amenities at each park, so that they have a different appeal and make the system more dynamic and interesting. The classification system (Class I, II, and III) refers to the quality of the park amenities and defines the appropriate level of use.

When completing an open space inventory, it is important to note both the number and quality of each component/facility. This classification system (Table 14.2) allows a planner to identify how well each space in the system serves the broad needs of the community.

Passive Area Class I	Softball Class II
Passive Area Class II	Soccer Pitch(s) Class I
Passive Area Class III	Soccer Pitch(s) Class II
Turf Class I	Soccer Pitch(s) Class III
Turf Class II	Sand / Beach Volleyball
Trail Class I	Tennis Court(s) Class I
Trail Class II	Tennis Court(s) Class II
Trail Class III	Running Track
Natural Vegetation	Basketball Hoops
Trees / Shrubs	Toboggan Run
Formal Gardens	BBQ / Picnic Area
Fencing	Skating Area-Pleasure
Hard Court Area	Skating Area-Hockey
Informal Play Area	Shelter / Washrooms
Play Area (Creative/Adventure)	Water Fountains
Wading / Spray Pools	Skateboard Area
Water Park	Parking
Ball Diamond(s)	Skate Board Park I
Softball Class I	Skate Board Park II

Table 14.2 Components of the Open Space System

Classification	Standard	Supply	Year 2000 Pop. 8000	Supply Per Pop.	Year 2006 Pop. 9691	Status Of Supply	Year 2028 Pop. 12000	Status Of Supply
Neighbourhood Park	3.5ac/1000	30.94 a	28 ac.	+2 ac.	33.6 a	-2.6 a	42.0 a	-11.06 a
Tot lot /Playground	1/1500 pop.	6	5.3	-ok-		-1		-2
Community Athletic	4.5 ac/1000	15.0 a	36 ac.	-21	43.2	-28	54 a	-39
Community Passive	2.0 ac./1000	3.75 ac.	16 ac.	-12.25	19.2 a	-15.4	24 a	-20.25 a
Regional Special:	N/A							
-Regional Athletic		43.85 a						
- Landscaped area		.50 ac.						
-Ag. Society		7.6 ac.						
-Camp Grounds		2.0 ac.						
-Golf Course		137.8 a						
-Trail /Linear								
-Outdoor Leisure Pool								
Total	10 ac/1000	241.5 a		10.25 a		-46.1 a		-70.31a

Table 14.3 Open Space Supply, Standards, and Deficiencies

Step 4. Open Space Standards and Guidelines

The standards that are described herein attempt to reflect the goals and objectives for the local government parks and recreation services. Standards provide a systematic, consistent approach to planning for open space and reflect the quantity of open space needed and the levels and categories of open space that will meet the broadest range of needs in an equitable manner.

Every community is unique; therefore, the standards, supply, park components, and classification system will be unique. However, there are some generally agreed-upon planning principles that can guide the development of open space.

As an example, Table 14.3 outlines the open space standards developed for a medium-size community (Winkler, 2000). Three service levels were defined (neighborhood, community, and regional), and an inventory of the components that exist in each park type and classification was identified and measured against the community-specific standards established for this community.

Site	Space	Classification
1. Kinsmen	6.68 ac	Neighbourhood Park
2. Lions Park	6.51 ac	Neighbourhood Park
3. Parkland Elementary*	5.76 ac	Neighbourhood Park
4. Winkler Elementary*	5.62 ac	Neighbourhood Park
5. J.R. Walkoff School*	6.37 ac	Neighbourhood Park
6. Garden Valley Collegiate*	15.00 ac	Community Athletic
7. Winkler Rec Centre Site:	(65.23 ac)	
Approximate Component of site:		
Baseball complex (8 fields)	43.88 ac	Regional Athletic
Passive/Picnic Area	3.75 ac	Regional Passive
Ornamental/Aesthetic	.50 ac	Regional Landscape
Stanley/Ag. Society	7.60 ac	Regional Special
Camp Grounds	2.00 ac	Regional Special
Pool/Area Site	(7.50 ac)	Regional Athletic
8. Linear Trail System	XXX	Regional Special
9. Golf Course	137.84 ac	Regional Special
Total	**241.51 ac**	

* Adjacent to but not including school site-open space only)

Table 14.4 Inventory of Open Space in Winkler

This approach allows planners to identify areas of relative deficiency and take corrective action. It must be stressed, however, that these are flexible minimum standards. While standards are suggested for each park type, other factors may affect the most practical location for parks spaces. The amount and suitability of land may not always be available in areas of need, and as a result, standards should only serve as a guide, not an absolute.

Step 5. Open Space Inventory

An important part of the systematic approach to park development is to assemble a comprehensive inventory of existing open space and the components and features that exist at each site. In conducting the inventory, care should be taken to describe each site and include the space available, facilities and components on the site, quality of development, access to surrounding residents, potential for use, and future development opportunities.

Frequently, an athletic park will have fields and pitches that overlap and could interfere with each other during play. The inventory should note that these are shared facilities and be sure not to overrepresent the number of playable fields in the community. A sample (Table 14.4) lists the park sites in a medium-sized community (Winkler, 2000) and describes them by name, location, space, and classification. Each site is then plotted on a map (see Maps #3 and #4) for visual interpretation and analysis. An inventory provides the basis for analysis and assists in locating areas where there may be a deficiency of open space or where an apparent oversupply exists.

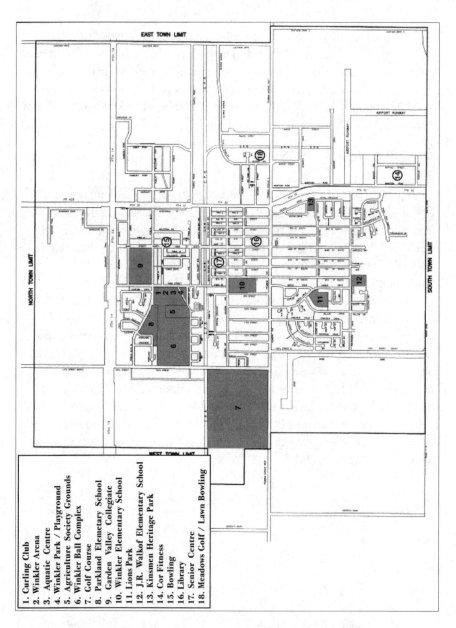

1. Curling Club
2. Winkler Arena
3. Aquatic Centre
4. Winkler Park / Playground
5. Agriculture Society Grounds
6. Winkler Ball Complex
7. Golf Course
8. Parkland Elementary School
9. Garden Valley Collegiate
10. Winkler Elementary School
11. Lions Park
12. J.R. Walkof Elementary School
13. Kinsmen Heritage Park
14. Cor Fitness
15. Bowling
16. Library
17. Senior Centre
18. Meadows Golf / Lawn Bowling

Map 3 Town of Winkler—Parks and Recreation Facilities Inventory

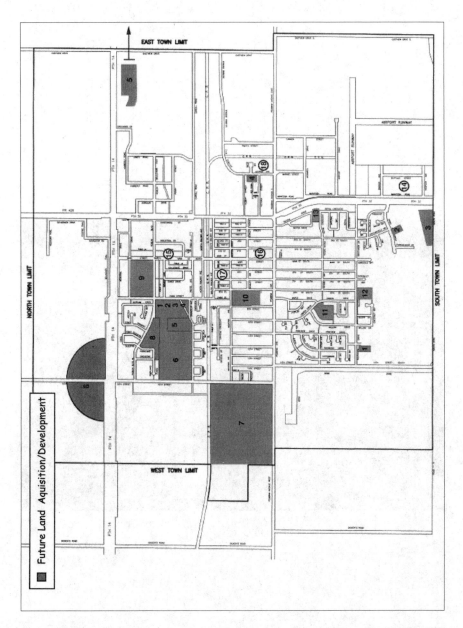

Map 4 Town of Winkler—Parks and Recreation Open Space and Park Sites

Section VI
Facility Operation and Maintenance

15.0 Maintenance Management Systems

15.1 Introduction

While the focus of this book has been on the predesign facility planning process, an equally important issue is the maintenance and upkeep of facilities once they are operational. Many of the major indoor facilities in Canada were constructed in the 1960s and 1970s during a major growth period in sport and recreation facility development. As a result, one of the major problems facing communities today is aging infrastructure and facility renewal. Few, if any, communities created reserve accounts to prepare for the cost of replacement of pools and arenas, and as a result, face major one-time budget expenditures for repair and replacement.

When new facilities are planned, it is important to carefully consider both the initial capital cost as well as the impact of the annual operating and maintenance costs over the long term. A new arena built by the public sector, for example, might cost $3 million to construct but due to the subsidized nature of the operation, an annual net operating cost of $600,000 each year for thirty years (on average) would cost $20 million over the life of the building. If adequate maintenance procedures are not implemented at the outset, the investment in the facility will be jeopardized.

There are many factors that affect the life expectancy of a building. Factors such as climate, location, design, quality of construction and materials, workmanship, type of use, and standards of maintenance will all affect the expected life of a building and its components.

Maintenance, like other management factors, must be carefully planned and managed. When financial resources are limited, maintenance often suffers as the day-to-day building use is the priority. Without long-term maintenance strategies, the life expectancy of a building and its components will be shortened.

15.2 Maintenance Defined

In the context of a recreation and parks operation, maintenance is described as the planned care and servicing of a facility or operating system to ensure its continued operation and function.

Maintenance is carried out for a number of important reasons. The standard of maintenance contributes greatly to the safety, comfort, and overall quality of the experience of facility users. In addition, maintenance improves the performance, efficiency, and life expectancy of the building and its components.

Maintenance falls into three categories, each with a specific purpose, and, therefore, a specific plan and process. Preventive maintenance is designed to detect possible system failures and prevent them with a planned response. If carried out successfully, preventive maintenance should ensure the life of a component or building up to and beyond its predicted life expectancy. Remedial or restorative maintenance is designed to restore a system or component to its original condition or replace the component, thereby allowing the facility to function as it was designed.

A third type of maintenance is described as routine maintenance that is carried out on a daily, weekly, or monthly basis, and while it is routine, it contributes to the life expectancy of the building as well as the comfort and safety of patrons.

Like other management functions, maintenance must be planned and executed within specific guidelines and rigorously monitored if the desired impact is to be achieved.

This chapter briefly explains two types of maintenance functions that have become common practice in most organizations that own, operate, and manage facilities. One is called PMMS or Planned Maintenance Management System and the other is referred to as life cycle planning. The sections that follow outline the process for each of these approaches.

15.3 Planned Maintenance Management System

Maintenance Management is a formalized asset management process designed to guide the proper maintenance of parks and facilities and protect the long-term capital investment of the community or asset owner. The process involves a number of well-defined steps, and its success relies heavily on the scheduling, control, and reporting process to ensure that

**Figure 15.1 Process for Designing a
Maintenance Management System**

the work is carried out as designed and targets are being met. Figure 15.1 illustrates the steps involved in the process.

1. Goals for the System

The first step is to collectively agree on the goals and targets that the system is seeking to achieve. The goals typically spell out the level of service desired and the operating principles around which standards are then established. The goals may be very broad and refer to the long-term quality, cleanliness, safety, and sustainability of the facility as well as promote both the efficient operation and effective delivery of services within the space.

2. Inventory of Facilities, Spaces, and Components

The next step is to conduct a comprehensive inventory of all spaces and their component parts to be maintained in the system. Indoor facilities and outdoor spaces have multiple operating components, and all must be included in the inventory and scheduled for attention.

Figure 15.2 illustrates an example of a facility and component inventory, and every park, playground, and facility in the system must have an inventory of its components and assets for the system to succeed.

3. Maintenance Standards

The standards of maintenance for each facility and component will vary based on the goals and targets to be achieved, the level, frequency and intensity of use, and the cost and benefits of each qualitative standard. For

FACILITY AND SITE INSPECTION REPORTS

BUILDING DESCRIPTION/ADDRESS   MAXIMO #

INSPECTOR   COMMUNITY CENTRE REPRESENTATIVE   INSPECTION DATE

NO.	GROUNDS	CHECK	NO.	BUILDING INTERIOR	CHECK	NO.	BUILDING MECHANICAL	CHECK
1	Contract Employee Ins.	√	25	Ceilings	√	47	Electrical: Switches/Plugs	√
2	Employee Workers Comp.	√	26	Walls	√	48	Lights/Exit	√
3	First Aid Kit	√	27	Entrance/Hallways	√	49	Fans/Supply/Exhaust	X
4	Fire Salary Plan	√	28	Stairways/Landings	√	50	Furnace Rooms	√
5	WHMIS Training	√	29	Floors/Mats	X	51	Furnaces/Filters	√
6	Fences/Signs	X	30	Doors/Windows	√	52	H. W. Tanks	√
7	Parking Lot	X	31	Signs/Furniture	√	53	Urinals/Toilets	√
8	Lighting		32	Storage Rooms	√	54	Sinks/Taps	√
9	Athletic Fields		33	Fire Exits	√	55	Emergency Light	√
10	Tennis Courts		34	Washrooms/Shower Room	X	56	Floor Drains	√
11	Hockey Pens	√	35	Basement	N/A	57	Healing Boilers	
12	Maintenance Calendar	√	36	Panic Dr. Hardware	N/A	58	Pumps	
13	Asbestos Status	√	NO.	CANTEEN/KITCHEN		59	Electric Motors	√
14	Occupancy Load	300	37	Stoves/Ranges		60	Time Clocks	√
15	MSDS		38	Refrigerator/Freezer		61	Thermostats	√
16			39	Electrical Appliances		62	Inc. Set Back	
			40	Exhaust Fan		63	Heat Detector	√
NO.	BUILDING EXTERIOR		41	Range Hood		64	Fire Extinguisher	√
17	Roof & Components	√	42	Deep Fryer		65	Sump Pump	N/A
18	Walls	√	43	Auto Fire Extinguisher		66	Backflow Preventer	
19	Doors/Windows	√	44	Fire Extinguisher		67	Electric Baseboards	√
20	Stairs/Rails/Ramps		45	Storage Shelves		68	Miscellaneous	X
21	Woodwork/Trim	√	46	Counter Tops		69	Light/Chain/Wire Guard	
22	Lights	√				70	Ceil. Fan/Chain/Wire Guard	
23	Signs	√				71		
24	Site Grading	√				72		

C. C. Responsibility	Description of Defect
49	Have all ductwork cleaned
25	Replace stained ceiling tiles in stairwells and hall areas
6	Service chain link fencing on West side
29	Clean storage room floor caused by 2nd floor kitchen
34	Patch hole in wall - main floor women's washroom

City Responsibility	Description of Defect
13	No asbestos at this facility
68	Investigate replacement of c. c. water service

Figure 15.2 Facility Inventory and Report Forms
(Source: Adapted from City of Winnipeg Facility Inspection Process)

example, high performance soccer players will require a higher standard of turf maintenance than mini soccer, and the greens of a golf course are mowed to a different standard than the fringe or the rough.

The standards for maintenance are developed on the basis of daily, weekly, monthly and annual requirements. In heavily used facilities, garbage would be removed every day, carpets might be cleaned monthly, and pools are shut down annually for major maintenance such as painting and tile replacement.

4. Costs and Budget

Each standard of maintenance will have different costs associated with the level of service provided. Typically, maintenance costs are predicted on the basis of unit cost projections that are suitable for annual budget preparation. For example, the unit cost of grass mowing would be estimated on a cost per acre or hectare basis, and the cost of garbage pickup might be estimated on the cost per hour for labor. For long-range budget purposes, a rule of thumb is to predict the annual operation and maintenance cost impact of a facility based on 3-5% of the initial capital costs of the facility.

5. Work Plans and Scheduling

Once the goals have been set, the components inventoried, and standards established, the next step is to develop a work plan that takes into account the budget available and the staff resources available to implement the plan. Typically the work plan assigns daily and weekly tasks to all personnel, and their time is then allotted to the tasks that need to be performed. Most staff work plans schedule approximately 80% of their time for routine maintenance functions, and 20% is left open for emergencies.

6. Performance Reporting

Reporting and evaluation are carried out by using computerized worksheets or checklists that are reviewed constantly to ensure compliance to the standards and schedule of duties. If assigned duties are unable to be completed, they are carried over to the next day, and the 20% set aside for emergencies will be utilized. The reporting process is the key function, because the results of the work plan will assist in modifying the standards, budget, and human resource requirements of the system

15.4 Life Cycle Management

Life Cycle Management is a proactive maintenance strategy to anticipate and predict when major parks and facility components will need to be. Recreation facilities are complex operating systems with multiple components and systems that break down and wear out. If the life expectancy of these components can be predicted accurately, a schedule for replacement can be established that minimizes the disruption of service to the public and the impact of the costs of major repairs spread over a longer period of time.

Life Cycle Management is intended to provide a long-range financial plan for the scheduled replacement of major components of parks and facilities. Once the predicted replacement dates have been established, regular facility inspections should continue as a normal part of an overall maintenance management process.

The steps in the process involve identifying the components of every facility that will likely need to be replaced within the lifetime of the building. Generally an inspection form is produced for each facility and component so that they can be easily tracked and accurate records kept. The forms should include (see Figure 15.3) basic information including the year the component was installed, the predicted life span of the component, and the replacement year forecast and cost.

The life span of a component can be obtained from manufacturers, facility maintenance personnel, or experience gained from the actual performance of systems over time. The life span is usually described as an average estimate, so regular inspections are required to validate predictions and budget accordingly.

The priority for each component is based on an assessment of the consequence of delaying replacement and the impact the delay will have

Facility: Pool   Constructed: 1967

Component	Yr. Inst.	Avg. Life Span	Year Replaced	Revised Replace Yr.	Cost ($)	Priority
Hot Water Heaters	1967	20	1987	2007	3	A
Boiler	1967	25	1992	2017	50	A
Motor Starters	1967	30	1997	2027	10	A
Security System	1985	15	2000	2015	10	B
Pool Tank	1967	35	2002		75	B
Lockers	1967	15	1992	2017	17	B
Utility: Water/Gas	1967	30	1997	2027	40	A
PA System	1985	15	2000	2015	10	C

Figure 15.3 Hypothetical Pool Life Cycle Forecast

on the facility and the users. Some components are essential to the operation of the facility (e.g., a boiler), and if not dealt with in a timely fashion, could result in closure. Other components could present a safety issue requiring immediate attention, while others are considered nonessential operating components and could wait while other priorities are dealt with.

As a facility ages, the replacement costs will grow as systems reach the end of their life cycle or become obsolete. A life cycle management process allows building owners to determine when the cost of repairs for the overall building are likely to exceed the replacement cost of the facility. After a facility has been in service for 50 to 60 years, it might be more economical to replace the building than continue to replace the operating systems one at a time.

One way that building owners can minimize the impact of excessive component replacement costs is to establish a reserve fund that is available when systems need replacement. A reserve fund can also minimize the impact of the capital replacement cost of a new facility when the time comes. It may be extremely difficult to find $3 million in one budget year to replace an arena or pool, and reserve funds spread the costs over an extended period of time. In the public sector, however, it is difficult for elected officials to set aside money for something that will be needed long after they have left office, but it is an important policy to consider as facilities and infrastructure age.

References and Resources

Alberta Community Development. (2000). A Look at Leisure #41: Favourite activities. Edmonton, Alberta.

American College of Sport Medicine. (1997). Health/Fitness Facility Standards and Guidelines (2nd ed.). Champaign, IL: Human Kinetics.

Balmer, K. (1988). Strategic planning – A simplified approach. (In: City of Calgary—Policy and Systems Plan). Calgary, Alta: City of Calgary.

Canada Fitness and Lifestyle Research Institute. (2004). Results of the 2004 Physical Activity Monitor and Report. Retrieved Feb. 15, 2007 from web site: www.cflri.ca/eng/statistics/index.php

Canada Fitness and Lifestyle Research Institute. (2004). 2004 Capacity Study- A Municipal Perspective on Opportunities for Physical Activity: Trends from 2000–2004. Retrieved Feb. 15, 2007 from web site: www.cflri.ca

City of Winnipeg. (2000). Plan Winnipeg 2020 Vision. Winnipeg, MB: City of Winnipeg.

Cordell, K. and Green, G. (2004). Participation Rates for Outdoor Activities in 2004. (Recreation and Tourism Update Report No. 1). Athens, GA: U.S. Forest Service.

Cordell, K. (2004). *Outdoor Recreation for 21st Century America*. State College, PA: Venture Publishing, Inc.

Daly, J. (2000). *Recreation and Sport Planning and Design* (2nd ed.). Champaign. IL: Human Kinetics.

Dillman, Don A. (2007). Mail and Internet surveys: The tailored design Method. Hoboken, NJ: John Wiley and Sons.

Dillman, Don A. (1978). Mail and Telephone surveys: The total design Method. Hoboken, NJ: John Wiley and Sons.

DmA Planning and Management Services. (2006). Innovative Sources of Funding for Development and Rehabilitation of Sport and Recreation Infrastructure. Mississauga, ON: Federal-Provincial/Territorial Sport Committee.

Edginton, C. R., Hudson, S. D., and Lankford S. V. (2001). *Managing Recreation, Parks and Leisure Services: An Introduction*. Champaign, IL: Sagamore Publishing.

Edginton, C., and Griffith, C. (1983). *Marketing for non-profit organizations*. Englewood Cliffs. NJ: Prentice Hall. (Adapted from Kortler, P. 168).

Farmer, P. J., Mulrooney, A. L., and Ammon, R. Jr. (1996). *Sport facility planning and management*. Morgantown, WV: Fitness Information Technology, Inc.

Flynn, R. B. (1993). *Facility planning for physical education, recreation and dance*. Reston, VA: American Alliance for Health, Physical Education, Recreation and Dance.

Fogg, G. E. (1992). *Park planning guidelines*. Ashburn, VA: National Recreation and Park Association.

Foot, D. K. (1996). *Boom, bust and echo*. Toronto, ON: Macfarlane, Walter & Ross.

Francis, M. (2003). *Urban open space: Designing for user needs*. Washington, MD: Island Press, Landscape Architecture Foundation.

Gardiner, P. (2007, Feb. 7). Kids Not Active Enough Study Says. *Winnipeg Free Press*, p. A4.

Godbey, G. (2006). *Leisure and leisure services in the 21st century— toward mid-century*. State College, PA: Venture Publishing, Inc.

Gold, S. M. (1980). *Recreation planning and design*. Toronto, ON: McGraw-Hill Book Company.

Haas, G. E. (2002). Visitor Capacity on Public Lands and Waters—Making Better Decisions. Ashburn, VA: National Recreation and Park Association.

Harper, J. and Somers, B. (2007, Feb. 16). Recreation Facility Master Plan. Brandon, MB: City of Brandon.

Harper, J. (2006). Feasibility Study—Bronx Parks/Good Neighbours Centre. Winnipeg, MB: Community Services, City of Winnipeg.

Harper, J. and Doyle, G. (2003). Strategic Development Plan, Burton Cummings Theatre. Winnipeg, MB: Walker Theatre Performing Arts Group, Inc.

Harper, J. (2000). Parks and Recreation Master Plan. Winkler, MB: Town of Winkler.

Harper, J. (1998). Parks and Recreation Master Plan. Altona, MB: Town of Altona.

Harper, J., Neider, D., and Godbey, G. (1996). The Use and Benefits of Local Government Parks and Recreation Services in Canada. Winnipeg, MB: Health Leisure and Human Performance Research Institute, University of Manitoba.

Hultsman, J., Cottrell, R. L., and Zales-Hultsman, W. (1987). Planning Parks for People. State College, PA: Venture Publishing, Inc.

Johnston, B. (1999). Illuminating Our Future—Parks and Recreation in Canada, Final Report and Proceedings. Ottawa, ON: Canadian Parks and Recreation Association.

Johnston, B. (1998). Major Recreation Facility Master Plan. Red Deer, AB: City of Red Deer.

Johnston, B. (1976). PERC priority rating. *Recreation Review, 5 (1)*, 53–57.

Kelsey, C. and Gray, H. (1996). Master Plan Process for Parks and Recreation (2nd ed). Reston, VA: American Alliance for Health, Physical Education, Recreation, and Dance.

Lutzin, S. G. (1980). Managing Municipal Leisure Services. Washington, DC: International City Management Association.

Manitoba Health. (2004). Population projections: Health assessment report to Manitoba Health. Winnipeg, MB.

Maslow, A. (1970). Maslow's Hierarchy of Needs. Motivation and Personality (2nd ed.). Toronto, ON: Harper & Row.

McLean, D. D., Bannon, J. J., and Gray, H. R. (1999). *Leisure Resources—It's Comprehensive Planning* (2nd ed.). Champaign, IL: Sagamore Publishing.

Mertes. J., and Hall, J. R. (1996). Park, Recreation, Open Space, and Greenway Guidelines. Ashburn, VA: National Recreation and Park Association.

Ontario Ministry of Culture and Recreation. (1976). Guidelines for Developing Public Recreation Facility Standards. Toronto, ON: Sports and Fitness Division.

National Recreation and Parks Association. (1983). Recreation, Park, and Open Space Standards. Ashburn, VA: National Recreation and Park Association.

Lee, N. D. (2004). Public Use Facilities Study. Winnipeg, MB: Department of Community Services, City of Winnipeg.

Ontario Ministry of Culture and Recreation. (1985). Planning Recreation: Manual of Principles and Practices, Toronto, ON.

Parks and Recreation Ontario. (2006). Physical Activity: For the Health of Canadians, Presentations to the Commission on the Future of Health Care in Canada. (In Investing in Healthy and Active Ontarians through Recreation and Parks Infrastructure, A Summary of Trends and Recommendation. Toronto, ON, Parks and Recreation Ontario.

Pena, W. M. and Parshall, S. A. (2001). *Problem seeking: An architectural program primer* (4th ed.). New York, NY; John Wiley and Sons, Inc.

Reid, D. (1998). Planning for the Changing Patterns of Work and Leisure, Manuscript submitted for publication.

Robinson, A. (2004). Leisure Trends Monitor. (Vol 1, Number 1). Ottawa, ON: Anne Robinson Associates.

Sawyer, T. H. (Ed.). (2005). *Facility design and management for health, physical activity, recreation, and sport facility development* (11th ed.). Champaign, IL: Sagamore Publishing.

Strachan, D. and Kent, J. (1985). *Long and Short Term Planning.* Gloucester, ON: Tyrell Press Ltd.

The United Way. (2002, September). Trends and Futures. Proceedings of Journey Forward, Winnipeg, MB.

Wright, J. R., Braithwaite, W. M., and Foster, R. R. (1976). *Planning urban recreation open space: Towards community-specific standards.* Toronto, ON: Ontario Ministry of Housing, Local Planning Policy Branch.

Zalatan, A. (1994). *Forecasting Methods in Sport and Recreation.* Toronto, ON: Thompson Educational Publishing, Inc.

Web and Related Resources

Manitoba Community Profiles: www.communityprofiles.mb.ca/

Statistics Canada: www.statcan.ca/menu-en.htm

Lifestyle Information Network: lin.ca

Governments of Canada & Manitoba
Interactive Business Planner
Canada Business Service Centre: www.cbsc.org/ibp

Appendices

Appendix A

Sample RFP—Request for Proposals

With Permission:

City of Regina, Community Services

Sincere appreciation to:

Louise Folk
Coordinator of Open Space and Facility Planning
Community Services Department
City of Regina

CITY OF REGINA

Request for Proposals

Consulting Services

Recreation Facility Strategy to 2020

RFP #1507

Closing Date: Wednesday, May 16, 2007

Closing Time: 2:00 p.m., CST

Table of Contents

A. Purpose

The Recreation Facility Strategy to 2020 will blend the City of Regina's corporate direction with a community needs assessment to determine the best model for the provision of municipal sport, culture, and recreation services in Regina. It will assess current sport, culture, and recreation needs of citizens and stakeholders, propose a vision for future services, outline a decision-making framework for service requirements, and recommend a recreation facility master plan to 2020.

The City of Regina is seeking proposals from qualified consulting firms to provide consulting in the area of sport, culture, and recreation strategic master plan development including:

- current state assessment
- development of a desired future state
- gap analysis
- facility recommendations to achieve the future state

Responses to this Request for Proposals (RFP) will provide the City of Regina with the information required to select a consultant to lead the development of a strategic master plan for sport, culture, and recreation services in Regina.

B. Eligibility

The consultant should specialize in strategic master planning in the sport, culture, and recreation field and have a track record demonstrating ability to successfully lead municipal governments in the development of recreation and facility service strategies. To be eligible to respond to this RFP, the consultant must demonstrate that it is a firm with significant experience in strategy development, research, needs assessment, citizen and stakeholder engagement, and recreation facility planning services. The consultant must demonstrate that it, or the principals assigned to the project, have successfully completed services similar to those specified in the Project Scope section of this RFP. Experience with sport, culture, and recreation best practices and trends, as well as citizen and stakeholder engagement, will be considered an asset.

The City desires to issue a contract to a single qualified consultant to lead a strategic master planning process for sport, culture, and recreation services in Regina. Consulting proposals based on a consortium approach, where more than one firm will provide support within a consulting team, are acceptable.

Proponents should be aware senior management has identified this initiative as a corporate priority for the City of Regina in 2007, and, funding for consulting services has been identified in the 2007 operating budget, which is expected to be approved by City Council in May 2007. The project is being lead by the Community Services Department and is in the initiation stage. A project charter has been developed by a steering committee and a project team has been identified. The consultant must demonstrate the project management methodologies he or she would apply in this context.

C. Background

The need for a Recreation Facility Strategy to 2020 is driven by the City of Regina's strategic focus on improving customer service and managing assets, coupled with shifting sociodemographics and citizen needs; emerging trends in sport, culture, and recreation; aging infrastructure; and the geographical growth of our city.

Over the past three years, the City of Regina has been engaged in a number of change initiatives. In 2004, a Core Service Review was completed and a continuum of services for our municipality was developed. In 2006, a new City Manager was hired and six strategic directions for the organization were identified. The organization is undergoing restructuring, preparing to embark on a corporate strategic planning process, and the development of a performance management system. Supplemental information is provided in Attachment 1, Corporate Context.

During the 1990s, the role of private industry and community-based organizations in the provision of sport, culture, and recreation programming and facilities has shifted. More and more, we are seeing an increasing number of private and community run facilities and program opportunities. Concurrently, municipalities across the country have been reevaluating their role in providing sport, culture, and recreational opportunities and activities in relation to legislated responsibility. This has resulted in the need to redefine municipal service frameworks for sport, culture, and recreation.

The last major recreational needs assessment and facility plan for Regina was completed in 1982. Since this time, a number of program and neighborhood specific plans have been developed, including Open Space Management Strategy (2007), 2003 Leisure Needs Assessment, The Athletic Field System (1996), and Core Neighborhood Sustainability Action Plan (2007). In addition to programming information, the City has begun to assess the condition of aging infrastructure. In 2004, facility audits for outdoor pools and arenas were completed. Supplemental information is provided in Attachment 2, An Overview of Regina's Sport, Culture, and Recreation Services.

Early in 2007, seven principles were developed by the project steering committee to inform and direct the development of this strategy.

1. Customer Focus—Community and stakeholder needs and requirements.
2. Flexibility—Adaptability to meet the various service delivery needs.
3. Consistency—Equitable access by way of fair and balanced distribution of service throughout the city.
4. Innovation—Being open to new ideas to achieve the goal of a sustainable service framework and facility infrastructure.
5. Engagement—Of residents, stakeholder, partners, and employees where input is important to determining future state or gaps in current service provision.
6. Communication—At all levels of the organization and throughout the community, to ensure that all stakeholders are aware of the initiative, the purpose, the activities undertaken, the results, and how it affects them.
7. Continuous Improvement—Open to challenging the status quo.

D. Submission Deadline

To receive consideration, responses to this RFP must be received no later than 2:00 p.m. Central Standard Time, Wednesday, May 16, 2007. Any proposals received after this time will not be considered.

One unbound original and eight copies of the proposal should be directed to:

City of Regina
Victoria Avenue
P.O. Box 1790
Regina, Saskatchewan
S4P XXX

Attention: XXXXXXX
Manager of Acquisitions
Telephone: (306) XXX-XXXX
Fax: (306) XXX-XXXX

Prior to the submission deadline, the City of Regina may amend or clarify the RFP. Any changes will be provided in writing to all proponents who originally received the RFP.

E. Withdrawal of Proposal

A proposal may be withdrawn at any time prior to the close of receipt of proposals.

F. Award

General

- The City will either award an appointment or announce that no appointment will be made. There is no implicit or explicit guarantee that the project will proceed. The City reserves the right to accept any or reject all proposals. In addition, the City reserves the right to seek clarification from and to negotiate with any or all proponents regarding their proposal.
- All terms and conditions of this RFP are deemed to be accepted by the responding consultant and incorporated by reference in its proposal, except for those that are expressly challenged by the consultant in its proposal.
- Proposals shall be firm from the time and date set for the receipt of proposals.
- The successful consultant is responsible for obtaining all necessary permits, licenses, and insurance at his own expense.

Agreement

- Any award resulting from this RFP is subject to the successful negotiation of an agreement between the City and the successful consultant. The contract will be governed by and interpreted in accordance with the laws of the Province of Saskatchewan. A sample of the City of Regina's standard consulting agreement is attached to this document as Attachment 3, City of Regina, Standard Consulting Agreement. The successful proponent will be required to enter into a consulting agreement with the City of Regina, based on this standard agreement.

- This RFP and the information provided within will become part of the agreement and be incorporated by reference.
- The successful consultant's proposal will form part of the contract.
- Claims made in the proposal or in any subsequent verbal or written presentation shall constitute contractual warranties. Any disputes shall be resolved in accordance with the following documents, which are listed in priority: a) the contract; b) the RFP; c) the accepted proposal.

G. Confidentiality

The city anticipates that the proponents may wish to treat certain elements of their submissions as confidential or proprietary. Proponents are advised, however, that freedom of information requirements in force in the Province of Saskatchewan may afford rights of production or inspection at the application of third parties. Further, the contract entered into by the successful consultant will, by law, be available for inspection by members of the public.

H. News Release

Proponents must not make public announcements or news releases regarding this RFP or any subsequent award of contract without the prior written approval of the City of Regina.

I. Incurred Costs

The City of Regina will not be liable in any way for any costs incurred by proponents in replying to this RFP.

J. Project Administration

The City of Regina has assigned project administration responsibilities for this project. If you require further information about this RFP please contact:

XXXXXXXX
Coordinator of Open Space and Facility Planning
Community Services Department
City of Regina
Regina, Saskatchewan

S4P 3C8
Telephone: (306) XXX-XXXX
Fax: (306) XXX-XXXX
Email: XXX@regina.ca

Contacts are restricted to the person identified above. Proponents are encouraged to obtain a clear understanding of the requirements, prior to completing proposals.

The City assumes no responsibility or liability arising from information obtained in a means other than those prescribed in this RFP.

K. Project Scope

The project is intended to clarify the municipal mandate and purpose for providing sport, culture, and recreational services. This will involve clarifying the City's philosophy and developing a policy and decision making framework for current and future service provision. Concurrently, this project will investigate and prioritize community and stakeholder needs and assess if our infrastructure is positioned to meet those needs.

In order to accomplish this work, the steering committee has identified six phases for the strategic master planning process. The phases of the project have been defined by a number of key questions. The City of Regina is expecting proponents to propose a methodology including proposed activities and deliverables to accomplish the strategic master planning process. Proponents should be aware the phasing and key questions outlined below are to be interpreted as a guideline for proposing methodologies.

- Phase I: What is our current state?
- Is it consistent with best practices, trends, and our environment?
- Phase II: What does the public think about our current services and key issues?
- Phase III: What is our future state?
- What are the key issues we need to address to get us to our future state?
- Phase IV: What gaps exist between current and future state? How will we deliver services in the future? What do we need to provide to meet community needs and achieve vision?
- Phase V: Does this plan meet community needs?
- Phase VI: How will we deliver services in the future? How will we implement and evaluate our plans?

The expected deliverables for the strategic master planning process include (but are not limited to):

- A community-based sport, culture, and recreation needs assessment
- A policy and decision making framework for determining future sport, culture, and recreation service provision for Regina to 2020
- A facility master plan for Regina to 2020 with recommendations that are prioritized, costed, and listed in a short-, medium-, and long-term timeframe

The scope of this project has been further defined in the following three sections.

1. Staff, Community, and Stakeholder Consultation Staff, community, and stakeholder consultation is a priority for this project. The City of Regina is expecting engagement to occur at various stages throughout this project. Proposed methodologies for identifying, mapping, and engaging a range of stakeholders including, but not limited to, decision makers, staff, community-based organizations, citizens, and user groups is expected.

2. Policy and Decision-Making Framework. The strategy will incorporate the following components of a policy and decision-making framework for City of Regina sport, cultural, and recreation service provision:

- Philosophy for service provision at the municipal government level
- Principles for service development at the municipal government level
- Priorities for service provision at the municipal government level
- Model or continuum for service provision at the municipal government level
- Community and stakeholder needs
- Decision-making framework linking service provision to corporate strategic planning and performance management
- Partnership and relationship opportunities for the provision

of services including, the development and assessment of these opportunities
- Emerging trends
- Best practices

3. Sport, Culture, and Recreation Facilities. The strategy will focus on indoor and outdoor facilities in the following service areas: athletic fields, aquatics, community facilities, culture, fitness, ice, outdoor sports complexes, speciality or destination facilities, as well as sport and play amenities. Focusing on these service areas, the intended outcome is a continuum of city-owned facilities in relation to facilities provided by other service providers in the community. We are expecting the continuum to align with strategies the City of Regina incorporates in open space planning and development charge funding, as well as a policy and decision-making framework for service provision. The scope does not include Regina Public Libraries.

L. Project Schedule

The general schedule to engage a consultant, subject to further consideration, is:

2:00 p.m., CST, May 16, 2007 – Proponents' response to RFP due.
May 2007 – Appointment of Consultant.
May 2007 – Work commences.

Note that proponents, in their proposal, are requested to outline an anticipated project schedule that reflects their recommended methodology for this project.

M. Proposal Format Requirements

Proponents should follow the proposal format outlined below. Please include key contact personnel in the event that more information is required. Additional information thought to be relevant, other than the categories listed below, should be provided as an appendix to the proposal.

1. Company Information

a. Provide company information:

- Name
- Address
- Telephone
- Email
- Key Contact
- Website

b. Provide a description of the consultant's business.

c. Provide summary information on the consultant's track record and accomplishments.

d. Provide a description of and contacts/references for at least three projects that have been completed by this consultant that are similar to this project.

e. Provide information indicating the extent to which this consultant is protected for professional liability.

2. *Technical Qualifications*

a. Describe the qualifications and expertise of the personnel who will be assigned to this project. Include a professional resume of each of the individuals who will be involved. Information provided should demonstrate capability for the following:
- Knowledge and experience developing strategic master plans for sport, culture, and recreation services delivered in an urban municipality
- Knowledge and experience in applying quantitative and qualitative research methodologies in the sport, culture, and recreation field
- Knowledge and experience in developing and facilitating engagement processes with a range of stakeholders including, but not limited to, decision makers, staff, community-based organizations, citizens, and user groups
- Knowledge of the sport, culture, and recreation delivery system, including the interaction between public, community-based, and private service providers
- Knowledge of best practices and trends in the sport, culture, and recreation field
- Knowledge of the governance structure and typical

functional structure of sport, culture, and recreation services operated by an urban municipality

3. *Approach*

a. Provide a general description of your understanding of the project.

b. Provide a general description of your understanding of the purpose of the project and outline the expected outcomes for the project.

c. Explain the methodology that would be used to complete the work. Be specific about the components of your methodology and provide information about what makes your methodology successful. Proponents should be aware that the most significant criterion for choosing a consultant is methodology (and related success with that methodology). Proponents are encouraged to be as specific as possible in this area of their proposal. Examples of some of the types of information that would be useful to the evaluation process include:

   • Description of the strategic master planning process you would bring to this project.
   • Description of the engagement process you would use for a range of stakeholders including, but not limited to, decision makers, staff, community-based organizations, citizens, and user groups.
   • Potential tools you would use during the planning process including, but not limited to, environmental scanning, stakeholder mapping and engagement, visioning, gap analysis, and evaluation of facility recommendations.
   • Description of components of a typical strategic master plan that you have developed (e.g., visioning, best practice and trends analysis, policy and decision-making frameworks, a facility master plan).
   • Include samples of completed strategic master plans that you have previously developed for other similar clients.

d. Describe the City's roles and responsibilities with respect to this project. Outline specifically the resource and time commitment that you would expect from the City.

e. Describe the engagement/project management model that would be used to communicate with, gather information from, and inform the City of Regina of your progress throughout the project. Include the various components of the process. Be specific about the types of interactions, frequency of such, and requirement for deliverables from the City.

4. Time Frame

a. Project schedule.

b. Provide information on specific project milestones and amounts of time to be spent in the following categories: (Please adapt the table below to meet your needs—at a minimum, this section of your response should include responses as outlined.)

	Anticipated Amount of Time to be Spent (days)	Milestone Date
Project start date	n/a	
Project plan		
Current state assessment		
Development of a desired future state		
Gap analysis		
Facility recommendations		
Composing the strategy document		
Delivery of finalized strategy document		

5. Fees, Charges, and Financial Structure

a. Provide pricing information for the project. All pricing should be quoted in Canadian funds. Proponents are required to build into their estimates any administrative fees, travel costs, insurance costs, licensing costs, Saskatchewan Workers' Compensation Board fees, disbursements, or expenses that they may incur while completing their work. Proposals requesting payment for actual costs incurred by the consultant will not be considered. Only fixed, fee-based proposals will be considered.

b. For the purpose of evaluation of proposals, proponents are required to provide detailed information on projected costs and effort associated with the various procedures required to, at a minimum, develop a strategic master plan process for sport, culture, and recreation services, undertake the planning process, complete a community needs assessment, engage stakeholders, and assess if our current infrastructure is positioned to meet the future state. Information in this section should clearly reflect the methodology and time frames in Sections 3 and 4 above. At a minimum, proponents should provide the following:

	Est. No. Days of Work	Personnel Involved	Personnel Daily Rate	Travel Cost and Disburs.
Project plan				
Current state assessment				
Development of a desired future state				
Gap analysis				
Facility recommendations				
Composing the strategy document				

c. Describe the process for invoicing the City.

N. Evaluation of the Proposal

The following criteria and weights shall be utilized as a guideline in the evaluation of the proposals. Individual criteria have been assigned varying weights.

The selection committee will include the City of Regina's Steering Committee for this project. The proposals will be evaluated using the four criteria as outlined above. At the sole discretion of the selection commit-

Category	Weight (%)
Qualifications and experience	30
Methodology and deliverables	35
Project time frame	15
Project cost	20

tee, a short list of the highest scored proponents will be developed. Proponents included on the short list may be invited to an interview with the selection committee. That interview may include a requirement for the proponent to make a presentation to the selection committee. The intent of the presentations/interviews will be to allow the selection committee an opportunity to clarify any questions resulting from the initial evaluation.

After the presentations, the City will reevaluate the short-listed proposals using the same criteria and complete reference checks. The final selection will be based on the city's determination of the best scoring and most advantageous proposal.

Proponents are strongly advised not to prepare their proposal submission based on any assumption or understanding that negotiation will take place. Proponents are advised to respond to this RFP fully at the time of proposal submission.

Attachment 1 – Corporate Context

Over the past three years, the City of Regina has been engaged in a number of change initiatives. In 2006, a new City Manager was hired and Six Strategic Themes for the organization were identified. The organization is preparing to embark on a corporate strategic planning process and the development of a performance management system and is undergoing a reorganization.

1. Core Services Review

In 2004, a Core Services Review was completed and a continuum of services for our municipality was developed. The continuum is a "framework based on values, or a vision. The application of this framework helps the City confront the need to make choices in a more reasoned way."[1] The continuum ranges from core or essential services to less-core or discretionary services. Sport, culture, and recreation services fell in the middle to less-core range on the continuum. The continuum is presented below:

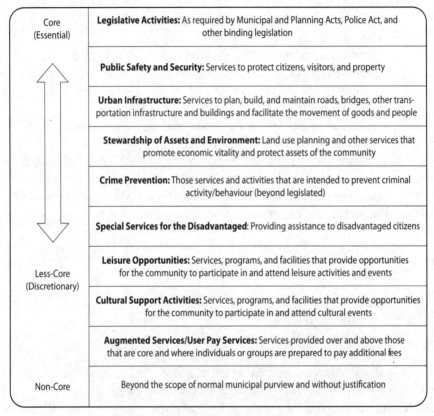

Core (Essential)	**Legislative Activities:** As required by Municipal and Planning Acts, Police Act, and other binding legislation
	Public Safety and Security: Services to protect citizens, visitors, and property
	Urban Infrastructure: Services to plan, build, and maintain roads, bridges, other transportation infrastructure and buildings and facilitate the movement of goods and people
	Stewardship of Assets and Environment: Land use planning and other services that promote economic vitality and protect assets of the community
	Crime Prevention: Those services and activities that are intended to prevent criminal activity/behaviour (beyond legislated)
	Special Services for the Disadvantaged: Providing assistance to disadvantaged citizens
Less-Core (Discretionary)	**Leisure Opportunities:** Services, programs, and facilities that provide opportunities for the community to participate in and attend leisure activities and events
	Cultural Support Activities: Services, programs, and facilities that provide opportunities for the community to participate in and attend cultural events
	Augmented Services/User Pay Services: Services provided over and above those that are core and where individuals or groups are prepared to pay additional fees
Non-Core	Beyond the scope of normal municipal purview and without justification

Working Definition of Core Services

2. Six Strategic Themes

In 2006, Six Strategic Themes were adopted by the senior management team with the endorsement of City Council to provide the framework for future strategic decision making.

1. Mandate—City Council and the Administration strategically determine which services the City provides, the level of service, service goals, and objectives for its programs.

---

1   *City of Regina/Regina Police Services-Core Services Review*, City of Regina, 2004, p. 20.

2. Asset Management—City Council and the Administration strategically and effectively manage assets within program areas to provide for economic, social, and environmental sustainability.
3. Service Delivery—City Council and the Administration make service delivery decisions that ensure the most effective and efficient service exists.
4. Revenue Generation—City Council and the Administration are committed to Corporate Revenue Strategy development and make revenue generation decisions based on clear, guiding principles.
5. Customer Service—City Council and the Administration are committed to the delivery of municipal services that meet the needs and expectations of customers.
6. Contemporary Employer—City Council and the Administration recognize that people are the organization's most valuable resource. Human Resource strategies work to achieve outcomes that best serve the organization and the community.

Further work in 2006 has led to priority focus on just three strategic themes:

1. Asset Management
2. Customer Service
3. Contemporary Employer

Using these three specific themes as a basis for decision making, the City's senior management team undertook priority-based decision making for 2007. The areas of focus for 2007 initiatives and resource allocations include:

1. Human Resource Initiatives
2. Investment in City Facilities
3. Customer Service Strategy Implementation
4. Major Recreation Facility/Programming Strategy
5. Collective Bargaining Strategy
6. Strategic Planning and Performance Management

In 2007, the City of Regina will embark on a corporate strategic planning process and develop a performance management system.

3. Organizational Structure

In June of 2006, the current City Manager commenced employment with this organization replacing an incumbent who worked in the position for nineteen years. A new organizational structure has been recommended for the organization and is currently being implemented. Nine departments are being transformed into five divisions, and the General Manager positions for each of the five portfolios are currently being filled. It is anticipated that these positions will be filled while this strategy is being developed, and at least one of the individuals appointed to these positions may play a significant role in this initiative. Level One and Two of the recommended organization structure are presented below:

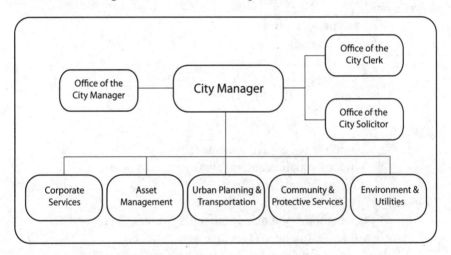

In addition, City of Regina managers are currently engaged in a functional alignment process with Blackstone Consultants. This process began in early 2007 and is expected to still be occurring as the Recreation Facility Strategy to 2020 is developed.

Attachment 2—An Overview of Regina's Sport, Culture, and Recreation Services

The Community Services Department provides a range of sport, culture, and recreation services to the community of Regina. In 2006, the city had a population of 185,010[2] and it is expected to grow to 209,600 by

2   *City of Regina, Saskatchewan Health Covered Population,* 1997 to 2006, Urban Planning.

2021[3]. Over the next ten years, development is expected to continue in the southeast and northwest, as well as begin in southwest Regina. In addition to growth in outlaying neighborhoods, efforts are under way to revitalize downtown Regina and inner-city neighborhoods such as Core and North Central. Revitalization efforts are focused on developing and implementing strategies aimed at achieving social and environmental sustainable communities.

The strategy will focus on indoor and outdoor facilities in the following service areas: athletic fields, aquatics, community facilities, culture, fitness, ice, outdoor sports complexes, speciality or destination facilities, as well as sport and play amenities. The City of Regina has the following facilities:

Athletic fields
- 94 athletic fields
- 179 diamonds
- 25 tennis sites (57 courts)
- 2 skateboarding facilities
- Leslie Lawn Bowling Greens

Aquatics
- 5 outdoor pools (average age 52 years)
- 3 indoor aquatic centers (average age 24 years)

Community Facilities
- 11 neighborhood and community centers (6 city and 5 volunteer operated) (average age 18 years)
- 2 senior citizen centers (both volunteer operated)
- Devonian Pathway

Culture
- Neil Balkwill Civic Arts Centre (24 years)
- Performing Arts Centre (volunteer operated)
- Floral Conservatory (volunteer operated)
- Arts Action Centre (under development)

Fitness
- Fieldhouse (19 years)
- 3 fitness rooms (located in indoor aquatic centers)

---

3   *City of Regina Source Book 2005*, Urban Planning Division, p. 2.1.

Ice
- 8 indoor ice arenas (average age 32 years)
- 23 outdoor boarded ice surfaces
- 42 outdoor pleasure ice surfaces
- 2 outdoor pleasure skating lake sites
- 1 outdoor speed skating oval

Sports Complexes
- Mosaic Stadium at Taylor Field—artificial turf field, fine turf practice field, and stadium seating for approximately 27,500 people
- Douglas Park—track and field amenities, athletic fields, and a cricket pitch
- Mount Pleasant—athletic fields and a speed skating oval

Sport and Play Amenities
- 145 play structures (approximately)
- 30 outdoor basketball sites
- 14 spray pads (aquatic)

Key Issues

Asset Management—City Council and the Administration strategically and effectively manage assets within service areas to provide for economic, social, and environmental sustainability. The City of Regina is faced with aging sport, culture, and recreation facilities. Budget constraints during the last decade have resulted in the deferring of maintenance costs. This has resulted in an infrastructure that is in need of retroversion or reconstruction. Policy- and decision-making frameworks are required to strategically guide and effectively manage sport, culture, and recreation assets

Customer Service—City Council and the Administration are committed to the delivery of municipal services that meet the needs and expectations of customers. A key consideration is assessing the needs and expectations of customers within the context of shifting sociodemographic trends, such as increasing first nations and senior populations. A clear understanding of community needs is required to ensure sport, culture, and recreation service provision is positioned to meet current and future community needs.

Service Delivery—City Council and the Administration make service delivery decisions that ensure the most effective and efficient service exists. Sport, culture, and recreation services are not currently structured to reflect best practices in the field. Best practice and trend information is an important component in the service strategy as it can facilitate effective and efficient service delivery. There are a number of current initiatives occurring in Regina that may inform, or be informed by, the service delivery model; for example, the Regina Exhibition Association Limited is in the process of developing a revitalization strategy for IPSCO Place, including the proposed development of 6 multipurpose arenas.

Documents Available to Consultant

- Open Space Management Strategy (2007)
- Assessment and strategy document for open space in Regina.
- Core Sustainability Action Plan (2007)
- This document is in the process of being developed. It is the result of a community-based, interdisciplinary, and multiagency approach to neighborhood planning.
- City of Regina, Saskatchewan Urban and Rural Golf Market Research Report Summary (2006)
- A market assessment for golf services in the Regina market by FAST CONSULTING.
- Recreation and Physical Fitness Study (2007)
- In partnership with Ipsos Reid, the research was focused on assessing citizens' physical activity levels and recreation behaviors and needs.
- Facility Audit: Pasqua Neighborhood Centre (2006)
- Facility condition and life cycle audit of one of the City of Regina's 11 neighborhood centers
- City of Regina Source Book (2005)
- Sociodemographic information for Regina by neighborhood and zone-based on 2001 Census data
- Core Services Review: Choices for Redefining Excellence (2004)
- Evaluation of municipal services for the City of Regina and the Regina Police Service
- Outdoor Ice Program Review (2004)
- An evaluation of the existing outdoor ice program and identification of program options for providing a base level of service and encouraging community involvement in the

operation, maintenance, and supervisio
- Facility Audits: Indoor Ice Arenas (2004)
- Facility condition and life cycle audit of the City of Regina's eight indoor ice arenas by NDLEA
- A Market Study for Regina's Indoor Arenas (2004)
- The research was conducted to collect information for developing an indoor arena capital plan and for evaluating current programs, services, and relevant policies.
- Facility Audits: Outdoor Swimming Pools (2004)
- Facility condition and life cycle audit of the City of Regina's five outdoor pools by NDLEA
- Leisure Needs Assessment (2003)
- Results of a leisure needs assessment survey conducted for the City of Regina by FAST CONSULTING. The survey assessed leisure and recreation habits, benefits or reasons for participating, and barriers residents face in participating in activities.
- Market Information on Regina's Outdoor Rink Sites (2003)
- An analysis of participation in outdoor rink activities in Regina during the 2002/2003 season
- Public Use of Regina's Outdoor Tennis Courts (2003)
- An analysis of supply and demand for court time
- Regina Development Plan, Part A, B, C, D (2001)
- The City of Regina's Urban Planning Division coordinates the development plan. The plan has many components, including policies related to projected growth and land use, such as park and recreational spaces, as well as sector plans for sectors of the City and neighborhoods.
- Facilities Analysis, City of Regina, University of Regina (2000)
- Indoor and outdoor facility inventory of City of Regina and University of Regina properties. Prepared by Ellard Croft for internal discussion in preparation for 2006 Canada Summer Games.
- The Athletic Field System (1996)
- Assessment, classification, and strategy document for athletic fields in Regina
- Discussion Paper: PERC Study Review (1994)
- Summarized city initiatives since the PERC study was undertaken in 1982 and recommended a review of the PERC study in the context of these new initiatives.

- Athletic Field Inventory and Evaluation (1993)
- Inventory and evaluation of athletic fields that was used as the base for The Athletic Field System (1996)
- Outdoor Pool Facility Study (1993)
- Facility condition and life cycle audits for the City of Regina's five outdoor pools by IKOY Architects
- A Review of the 1982 Major Recreation Facilities Study (1988)
- Implementation status of the recommendations in the 1982 study and recommendations on how to proceed with capital planning for the next 10 years
- The Outdoor Ice Surface Report (1987)
- A Recreation Program Policy Plan (1986)
- Defines the role of the Parks and Recreation Department, a delivery system for recreation program services, a program management policy, and the role of collaborative relationships. Prepared by Jack Harper and Associates.
- PERC Study (1982)
- The purpose of the study was to provide a framework for the development of major recreation and cultural facilities and services in Regina for 10 years. The study included three components: major facilities, leisure behavioral profiles, and special emphasis on recreation services to Regina residents of First Nations ancestry.
- Other City of Regina documents, including the following:
  - Operating and Capital Budget Documents
  - Parks and Recreation Development Charge Funding Criteria and Projected Projects to 2031 (2006)
  - The Southwest Sector Open Space Guiding Principles (2006)
  - Draft-Southwest Sector Proposed Recreational Facilities (2006)
  - Notes for Sports Event Congress (2006)
  - Omnibus Survey Results (2006)
  - Accessible Playground Report (2003)
  - Bike Network Study (2002)

APPENDIX B

Facility Assessment Process—A Checklist

Indoor Facility Evaluation Format

I. General Information (if available)

Name and address of facility
Name of Agency that owns/manages the facility
Date facility was constructed
Total indoor area of the facility (square footage)
Total outside acreage of the facility
Capital costs
Process involved in the planning of the facility

II. Site Selection/Suitability

Context of building and surrounding area
Accessibility (public/private transportation)
Visibility and signage
Parking (auto/bike)
Land value (relative)
Available space/potential to expand
Proximity/service radius
Environmental conditions
Aesthetics
Site constraints

III. Facility Status

Purpose and objective of the facility
Description of the facility and components, including accessibility
Current condition, appearance, and maintenance of the facility
Capacity to accommodate use/spectators
Current use, users, and uses
Relationship to qualitative and quantitative standards

IV. Additional Information

Include information related to operating costs, user fees, facility policies,
program information, and any additional information that is unique to this
facility.

V. Summary

Develop a summary assessment of the facility. Describe how it meets current goals and demands, outline deficiencies that you have identified, and comment on the adequacy of the planning process used for the facility.

VI. Diagram the Facility

The diagram does not have to be to scale but must include all areas of the facility.

Outdoor Facility Evaluation Format

I. General Information

Name and address of facility
Name of Agency that owns/manages the facility
Date park/area was constructed
Total acreage of the park/area
Capital costs/land values

II. Site Selection

- Context of park / facility and surrounding area
- Accessibility (public/private transportation)
  - Accessibility for special needs users: How have the facilities been built/modified to meet the needs of those with special needs? (Wheelchair ramps, water fountains, bathrooms, signage, handrails, etc.)
- Visibility and signage
- Parking (auto/bike)
- Land value (relative)
- Available space / potential to expand
- Proximity / service radius
- Environmental conditions:
  1. Topography: Describe the park/area topography (level, sloping, hilly, etc.)

2. Prevailing winds and natural barriers: Identify the prevailing wind direction and any natural barriers (trees, hills, dells)
3. Hydrology: Identify the presence of surface and/or subsurface water and the drainage pattern of any water present
4. Annual climate: Describe the monthly precipitation, temperature high/low

- Aesthetics and environmental concerns: Identify the proximity of the park/area to outside sound/sights/air quality, etc.
- Site constraints

III. Facility / Park Status

- Purpose and objective of the facility / park
- Description of the park/facility and all components (service/ maintenance/concession)
- Current condition, appearance, and maintenance of the facility
- Capacity to accommodate use/ spectators
- Current use, users, and uses
- Relationship to qualitative and quantitative standards

IV. Environment and Control Systems

a. Surface: Describe the materials used to construct any roadways, sidewalks, bike/horse paths, and ATV paths.
b. Signage: Identify the location and types of signage used and the materials used to construct the signs.
c. Lighting: Identify the types, locations, and illumination (foot-candle) of all lighting used in the park/area.
d. Barriers: Identify the types, locations, and materials used to construct any travel (car, pedestrian, bike, horse, etc.) barrier used in the park/area.
e. Fencing: Identify the types, location, and materials used to construct any fencing used in the park/area.
f. Utilities: Describe the types of utilities (electrical, water, sanitation, drainage, communications) present in the park/area.

g. Turf: Identify the dominant turf (class I, II, or III) present in the park/area.

h. Trees/Shrubs: Identify the dominant types of trees and shrubs within the park/area.

i. Animal Inventory: Identify the animal and bird species which live within the park/area. Also list any concerns relating to the animals' habitat or behavior that may impact the park operation.

Sample Park Components

Passive Area Class I
Passive Area Class II
Passive Area Class III
Turf Class I
Turf Class II
Trail Class I
Trail Class II
Trail Class III
Natural Vegetation
Trees/Shrubs
Formal Gardens
Fencing
Hard Court Area
Informal Play Area
Play Area (Creative/Adventure)
Wading/Spray Pools
Ball Diamond(s)
Softball Class I
Softball Class II
Soccer Pitch(es) Class I
Soccer Pitch(es) Class II
Soccer Pitch(es) Class III
Sand Volleyball
Tennis Court(s) Class I
Tennis Court(s) Class II
Running Track
Basketball Hoops
Toboggan Run
BBQ/Picnic Area
Skating Area—Pleasure
Skating Area—Hockey

Shelter/Washrooms
Water Fountains
Skateboard Area
Parking

VII. Additional Information

Include information related to operating costs, user fees, facility policies, program information, and any additional information that is unique to this facility.

VIII. Summary

Develop a summary assessment of the park / facility. Describe how it meets current goals and demands, outline deficiencies that you have identified, and comment on the adequacy of the planning process used for the facility.

IX. Diagram the Facility

The diagram does not have to be to scale but must include all areas of the park/facility.

APPENDIX C

PERC Priority Rating System—City of Red Deer Case Study

The City of Red Deer
Major Recreation Facility Master Plan
1998
(With Permission: Brian Johnston, Professional Environmental Recreation Consultants Limited)
Facility Priority Ranking – An Excerpt from the Study

Section 6.0 The Wish List

The public survey, interest group interviews, analysis of the existing inventory of facilities, and review of planning studies all point to a list of twelve types of space which are in demand in Red Deer. That is not to say that all twelve will be built. Further analysis is required. However, the spaces on the so called wish list need to be clearly defined so as to be able to do the further analysis. The spaces are defined in subsequent sections. It should be noted that the spaces are listed in no particular order.

6.1 Competitive Aquatics

There is no indoor pool in Red Deer adequate to hold high-level, long-course (i.e., 50 meter) swim meets, synchronized swim competitions, or diving competitions. Also the speed swimming clubs, the synchronized swim club, and the new diving club (started in September 1998) have expressed their demand for higher quality training facilities in order to increase the level of skill and competition in their respective sports. Collectively these clubs and programs comprise approximately 300 participants, many of which would benefit from better competition facilities for aquatics in Red Deer.

The facility which would meet this demand would be a 50-meter, long rectangular tank with a large deep end suitable for diving, water polo, and synchronized swimming. An ideal tank would have the following features:

- 8-lane-wide tank by 52-meter long to allow for a moveable bulkhead—52-meter by 20-meter or 1040 square meters of water surface area
- sufficient deck space to accommodate high volumes of swimmers, coaches, and officials in a competition situation— another 700 square meters of deck space
- one- and three-meter springboards and three and five-meter diving towers

- depth of 3.8 meters to accommodate platform diving
- whirlpool for warming up and warming down divers
- spectator seating area (either permanent or portable seating)
  for up to 900 spectators—approximately 600 square meters
- warm-up and cool-down lanes to support the main pool tank
  during high-level meets are also a requirement—a minimum
  of six 25-meter lanes would allow for meets up to and
  including some national level meets—another 700 square
  meters, including the deck area around the warm up tank
- dressing rooms and showers to accommodate up to 500
  patrons (the practical maximum number of swimmers in the
  two tanks) would add a further 600 square meters of space
- mechanical, electrical, storage, first-aid room, staff areas, and
  maintenance areas would add a further 400 square meters of
  space.

The total of all the above spaces would be approximately 4500
square meters. The capital cost of such a facility including all fixtures,
furnishing, design fees, parking areas, and site work, would be about
$12 million in 1998 funds. If the warm-up tank were not included in
the project (i.e., financed separately or already existing), the capital cost
would be reduced to about $9 million. It would have an annual functional
capacity of about 800,000 swims in a typical multiuse 110-hour per
week operating format. It would be able to serve a wide variety of uses
including fitness swimming, learn-to-swim programs, sports training, and
sports competitions. Given that the current three pools in Red Deer accommodate 250,000 swims annually and have some excess capacity, it is
unrealistic to expect that a new 50-meter competition tank would operate
at more than 50% of capacity in the near-term future. At that level of use,
the annual operating deficit (i.e., the proportion of operating costs not
covered by uses, but financed by taxpayers) would be about $1,000,000
(reduced to about $700,000 if the warm up tank is not part of the project).
In addition to these amounts, there would be an extra $100,000 per year
of added deficit in the two city operated pools due to transfer of uses from
those facilities to the new pool.

6.2 Leisure Aquatics

The public survey reinforced the interest in recreational swimming and
therapeutic swimming. A great many citizens feel that they would like
better facilities to meet these interests. Such a "leisure pool" would be a

free-form tank primarily with warm shallow water and would include the following features:

- main tank with area of approximately 400 square meters of water surface area with depth from zero to 1.5 meters with rapids channel, conversation bubble pits, and water play structures, suitable for fitness programs, therapeutic programs, recreational play, water orientation for new swimmers, and some swim instruction
- deck area to support leisure tank including games area—total about 500 square meters
- whirlpool with conversation pits—total of about 50 square meters, including deck area
- sauna and steam areas—total of another 50 square meters
- water slide with its own runoff area—total 50 square meters
- dressing rooms, including privacy cubicles for people with disabilities and families—to serve a total functional capacity of about 300 patrons—total 550 square meters
- mechanical, electrical, staff, circulation, and control areas, storage areas, and other miscellaneous support areas would total about 600 square meters

This component would total about 2200 square meters of space and would cost about $5.5 million to develop, inclusive of all soft costs, site development costs, and overheads. This facility would generate a number of new uses and users because of its attractiveness. It would also be more cost-effective to operate than the competition pool because of the relatively low water volumes in relation to high usage levels. It is reasonable to expect that the facility would operate with an operating deficit of about $250,000. However, it would cause an increase in operating deficits of the other two city-operated indoor pools of another $100,000, for a total impact of about $350,000 per year (i.e., about $6 per resident of the city).

6.3 Leisure Ice

Leisure ice is a relatively new concept in western Canada. Only a few communities have developed such facilities (e.g., Grande Prairie AB, Abbotsford BC, and Taylor BC). However, leisure skating facilities are becoming popular in other parts of the world, and wherever they have been developed, have been highly successful. The results of the public survey suggest that a high-quality public skating experience is in great demand. Low participation in existing arenas suggests that they are not meeting that demand. A leisure ice sheet is an attempt to provide a quality environment for public skating, learn-to-skate programs, patch skating by figure skaters, and some drill practice areas for all ice users. A leisure ice area would include a free-form ice sheet with the following characteristics:

- about 800 square meters of space in a high quality pleasure skating environment
- fireplace and other amenities for socializing and lounging associated with the skating experience
- informal spectating area totaling about 100 square meters.
- mechanical, electrical, storage, and other support spaces totaling another 150 square meters (more if developed alone without the sharing of support spaces with associated arena sheets).

The leisure ice module would accommodate up to 800 skaters per week over an average of 20 weeks per year, for a total of about 16,000 uses per year. The total of 1100 square meters of space would cost about $2.1 million to develop, including all overhead, soft costs, and all site work. It would not operate effectively without one or more adjacent ice arenas because of the economies of scale in equipment and labor. If, however, other ice spaces are provided, the leisure ice would require only about $50,000 of operating subsidy per year.

6.4 Ice Arenas

Ice user groups have indicated that up to two arenas could be added to the existing supply of five participant oriented ice sheets in Red Deer to sat-isfy demand for more practice time and game time for ice sports includ-ing hockey, figure skating, speed skating, and skating programs. School officials also indicated that more ice time would help them in scheduling school use of arenas during school hours. A total of about 100 hours of ice time per week is currently purchased by Red Deer ice user groups in surrounding communities like Sylvan Lake, Lacombe, Innisfail, and Blackfalds. This represents about one more ice sheet (or more if that time is accommodated all in prime time). Satisfying that ice time in Red Deer would negatively impact those surrounding facilities by taking revenue from them. However, it would make for increased convenience for the ice users that would be able to use facilities closer to home. Ice users identi-fied a need for two ice sheets as follows:

- one regulation NHL sized ice sheet about 27M by 60M with spectator capacity for about 200 people
- one Olympic sized ice sheet about 30M by 60M with spectator capacity for about 600 people
- ten dressing rooms to accommodate users of both genders totaling another 300 square meters
- circulation, control, storage, mechanical, electrical, and other support spaces totaling about 1000 square meters

This element of the building would comprise about 5800 square meters of space and would cost about $7 million to develop inclusive of all design fees, other soft costs, site work, and furnishings. The two arenas are considered as a single unit because of the economies of scale in operation and development. However, one arena and the leisure ice module may also provide similar economies of scale. They would require at least $200,000 in annual operating subsidies and would create a further $50,000 deficit in other city-operated facilities, as off-peak time in those spaces is shifted to better ice times in the new facilities.

6.5 Multipurpose Fieldhouse

A number of user groups in interviews and the general public in the survey indicated strong support for a new, large, clear span, high ceiling, dry floor space suitable for a wide variety of uses. Expressed demand included two indoor soccer fields, any number of indoor tennis courts, field practice area, running, walking, jogging track, and a special event venue. The following characteristics of space would come closest to satisfying all the above demand:

- room for two indoor soccer fields with removable perimeter boards and multipurpose flooring, each 25M by 55M, for a total area of about 3000 square meters
- multipurpose space for indoor tennis and spectating for special events adjacent to the soccer field spaces—another 2000 square meters
- ten change rooms and public washrooms totaling another 300 square meters
- other support spaces including mechanical, electrical, storage, administration, and janitorial, totaling a further 400 square meters
- A 300-meter-long walking, jogging, running (but not competition) track totaling 1700 square meters

- Spectator support services, including circulation and control, totaling another 1000 square meters
- Most, if not all, of the clear span areas with high ceiling, up to a maximum of 12M.

With careful "stacking" of spaces and efficient use of space, the total building would be about 7500 square meters on a footprint of about 6000 square meters. It would cost approximately $7.5 million to develop including all associated costs. The space is relatively efficient to operate, and with demand for use so high, it is conceivable that it would be used to more than 90% of available capacity. That would allow the facility to break even from an operating point of view. It would be used during the day by school groups and other drop-in users. It would be used during out-of-school hours by sports groups renting space, by individuals dropping in, and for some programs sponsored by the city.

6.6 Gymnastics Gym

The Red Deer Gymnastics Club has operated a dedicated gymnastics facility for over 20 years. The group has grown to a point where it has over 600 club members at all levels of skill from beginner to elite athlete. The facility, which the club has leased, includes a dedicated 750-square-meter gym, a preschool area of about 100 square meters, and support spaces, totalling another 150 square meters. The club is required to find new premises and is looking for a larger facility to accommodate current and future needs. Ideally, the club is interested in a gymnastics area as follows:

- dedicated gymnastics gym of about 1200 square meters for training and skill development, with a ceiling in at least part of the gym at least 11M high
- spectator area of about 15 square meters for parental viewing
- dressing rooms, showers, and washrooms, totaling another 150 square meters
- administration and storage space comprising about 150 square meters

The above space would allow the club to grow into the roughly 50% more space than it now has (net of the preschool space). In addition, it would like to have access to a preschool program area to operate this very successful program. That space is described under another heading in this list, but could and should be operated by the Gymnastics Club if properly located in the complex so as to be physically adjacent to the gymnastics gym, as it is in the existing facility. The 1550 square meters would cost approximately $2.2 million to develop, including all overhead and soft costs. The Gymnastics Club has shown that it is capable of operating such facilities on a user-pays basis with no requirement for a public operating subsidy.

6.7 Preschool Program Areas

There appears to be demand by local groups and the general public for some sort of dedicated space serving young people. This could be a full-time licensed day care, a part-time regular preschool, a programming space for one-off programs for young people, a drop-in play space, or a babysitting service while parents are in other parts of the complex. In fact, it could be any or all such services. Depending on the service, the size of this module of space might vary. However, for the purpose of initial discussion, it could include the following features:

- a central program area in which programs and services are based, say about 175 square meters
- a dedicated play area with fixed equipment—another 100 square meters
- support areas to serve the above with specially fitted washrooms and administrative area—totaling another 100 square meters

Such a space could be operated by the Gymnastics Club or any other agency serving young children in Red Deer. The total area of about 375 square meters would cost approximately $.5 million to develop. It could likely be operated on a break-even basis.

6.8 Multipurpose Areas

A number of interest groups indicated the need for multipurpose spaces for their activities and as support areas for their activities in other spaces. Although the two high schools on the site have a number of spaces which could be accessible for these uses, a small amount of multipurpose space is needed within the new recreation complex directly adjacent to other spaces. A total of three spaces could be provided of different size and level of finishing as follows:

- A 280-square-meter rectangular space for programs, special events, and group rentals—would have a hard-wearing floor surface suitable for activities like fitness programs, preschool games, meetings, etc.
- A 170-square-meter space with sprung hardwood floor, barres, and wall mirrors suitable for fitness classes, dance programs and classes, combative programs and other active uses
- A 100-square-meter space suitable for a wide variety of activities, including possibly a fitness/wellness area or other active uses
- A 30-square-meter space finished as a board room for meetings, temporary offices, and other small gatherings

These spaces, totaling about 580 square meters, would act in concert with other modules of space during events (e.g., as an administrative center and preparation area during tournaments and competitions) and as stand-alone activity spaces when the school spaces are being used. Without such spaces, the size of some other spaces (e.g., the preschool program area) would have to be enlarged. The cost of developing such space would be about $.8 million. They would operate on a break-even basis or require a very small subsidy.

6.9 Swing Center

There is some demand for a variety of teaching and practice space for activities which are linear in their orientation. Some comment from the public survey and some demands from interest groups point to the need for some long, narrow bays of space which could flexibly be configured for golf swing, batting practice, pitching practice, tennis swing, and archery practice. This suggests a series of six to eight separate areas separated only by fencing or other transparent means of separating projectiles from each other. Each would be about 5M wide, 5M high, and about 20M long. With fencing gates, ball-throwing machines, netting, and other finishing materials, the spaces could be used by individuals renting a bay or half a bay for individual practice, by coaches drilling teams or individuals on skill development, by instructors conducting classes, or by groups arranging competitions. The total area would be about 700 square meters of roughly-finished space divided into long, narrow areas. It would be relatively inexpensive to develop due to the low need for finishing materials.

Development costs would approach $.5 million. The spaces would likely generate a minimal operating surplus.

6.10 Retail Space

Several groups indicated the desirability of a small amount of retail space in the new recreation complex to provide goods and services to support users of the spaces in the facility. Examples include soccer equipment, skating equipment and services, other sports goods and rental services, and general fitness supplies. Such spaces would likely be operated by a private company which would lease space in the center. A small amount of space is indicated; perhaps about 60 square meters located in a central, high-profile area of the complex. It would cost about $.1 million to develop and would operate at a surplus to the facility.

6.11 Food and Beverage Space

The two high schools on the site both have extensive food and beverage services for students. Providing much food and beverage service in a new recreation complex could compete with these two existing services to the detriment of all three. However, there is significant comment in the interest group interviews and the public survey that some form of food and beverage service is required to support users and uses of the new recreation complex. Users will not likely leave the building to go to an adjacent building for service, and the school venues will not be operating during out-of-school hours when demand in the recreation complex is greatest. Therefore, a modest food and beverage operation is provided in this wish list. It could be operated by a nonprofit organization, the private sector, or either of the two school-based food and beverage operators. A total of 90 square meters of space is included in this wish list for food and beverage service and consumption. It would be located centrally in the complex and focus on serving public users of the building. It would cost approximately $.2 million to develop and would operate at a surplus to the complex.

6.12 Summary of Spaces on the Wish List

Figure 16 summarizes the size and costs of the spaces described in the previous eleven subsections. It should be noted again that the order of spaces in the figure is not intended to indicate priority of the spaces.

Space	Size	Construction Cost in $M	Soft Costs in $M	Total Development Costs in $M	Operating Deficit in $000's
Competition Pool	4500	9.7	2.3	12	1,100
Leisure Pool	2200	4.0	1.5	5.5	350
Leisure Ice	1100	1.5	0.6	2.1	50
Ice Arenas	5800	5.0	2.0	7.0	250
Multipurpose Fieldhouse	7500	5.5	2.0	7.5	0.0
(indoor soccer fields)	(3700)	(2.7)			
(other multipurpose)	(2100)	(1.5)			
(indoor jogging track)	(1700)	(1.3)			
Gymnastics Gym	1550	1.5	0.7	2.2	0.0
Preschool Program Space	375	0.4	0.1	0.5	0.0
Multipurpose Spaces	580	0.6	0.2	0.8	0.0
Swing Centre	700	0.4	0.1	0.5	0.0
Retail Space	60	0.06	0.04	0.1	0.0
Food and Beverage Space	90	0.1	0.1	.2	0.0
Support Spaces for all of above	2200	2.5	1.0	3.5	250
Totals	5,555	$31.26M	$10.64M	$41.9M	$2,000,000

Figure 16 Summary of Spaces on the Wish List

Note: In the above figure, the construction costs include just the cost of building the space. Soft costs include all other development costs, including development permit applications, GST, parking, landscaping, design fees and disbursements, building fixtures, inflation to 1999, and a small contingency.

7.0 Criteria for Prioritizing the Items on the Wish List

Twelve criteria for assessing the priority of recreation spaces were identified in a focus group of community opinion leaders and ratified in a

Criteria	How it is Used to Set Priorities
1. Public Demand	The public survey provides an accurate profile of what the general public is thinking and wanting. It can be used to help set priorities.
2. Community Benefit	People we elect and appoint to make decisions on our behalf will interpret need and set priorities based on their interpretation of need. The values espoused in the Community Focus Group reflect a workable set of community needs.
3. Broad-Based Access	A public facility, by definition, should be available to everyone in the community. Therefore, facilities that have barriers to any segment of the public (e.g., by levels of skill or abillity, or age, or gender, or by setting too high a price, or by having to join a group) will be lower priority than spaces which are available to all.
4. Participant Oriented vs. Spectator Oriented	Attempts will be made to accommodate both spectators and participants because both have value to the community. However, if tradeoffs have to be made, spaces that accommodate participants will be given higher priority than spaces which serve spectators.
5. Serving Expanding Needs	Spaces which serve needs and demands which are growing will be considered higher priority than spaces which serve activities which are not. For example, spaces with demographic groups which are growing in proportion to the population will be high priority, as will spaces which serve long-term growth trends and spaces which serve promising new activities that meet other criteria.
6. Variety	Spaces which do not exist now and which will serve new markets will take precedence over spaces which duplicate existing spaces and which provide more service to those already receiving some.
7. Adaptable and Flexible	Spaces which are sufficiently adaptable that they can meet more than one need will be higher priority than single-purpose spaces. Also, spaces that can relatively easily be adapted over time if their use wanes will be considered higher priority than spaces which cannot easily be adapted to other uses over time.
8. Cost-Effective (both Capital and Operation)	Spaces which can do all of the above at significantly less cost than other spaces will be considered higher priority than those that require more public invest-ment per unit of public good received. In this analysis, both capital costs to the taxpayer and operating costs to the taxpayer will be considered, as will negative economic impacts on other public-supported facilities.
9. Optimization of Location	Spaces which make best use of the proposed site between the two high schools will be given priority over spaces which might be best located elsewhere or just as easily located elsewhere.

Figure 17 Criteria for Setting New Facility Priorities

workshop with elected representatives in October. The twelve criteria were synthesized into eight broad headings. The eight headings were en-dorsed by the second public forum, but participants at the forum added a ninth heading. The nine broad criteria are summarized in Figure 17.

As Figure 17 suggests, there was a lot of discussion about the dis-tinction between the terms "demand" and "need." The general agreement at the end of this discussion was that demand focuses on the direct ben-

efits to the users of the service. If people say they want a space, it is typically because they want to use it and are thinking about the direct benefits
they will derive from its use. When people say that a facility is needed
in the community, they are typically referring to the indirect benefits to
everyone in the community if the facility is built. In other words, they
believe that users and nonusers will benefit from it. According to this line
of reasoning, the private sector is "demand driven" (i.e., if there is sufficient demand for something, the private sector will provide it regardless
of whether there is any "public good" attached to it). On the other hand,
the public sector is "needs driven" (i.e., must always be focused on the
"greater public good" of a service or a project because all taxpayers are
paying for it and all must get some form of benefit from it regardless of
whether or not they use it directly). This line of reasoning would suggest
that the community benefit criterion in the above list of criteria is more
important than the demand criterion. However, if there is no demand for a
service, there is no use providing it. Some of the other criteria relate also
to need and community benefit as defined in this discussion.

8.0 Analyzing the Items on the Wish List

The twelve components of space on the so-called wish list were then
analyzed using the criteria endorsed in the public forum as outlined in the
previous section. Based on all data compiled in previous steps in the process, assumptions were made about the characteristics of space needed,
the costs of providing that space, levels of use, impact on existing facilities, operating format, degrees of community access, and amounts of public good. As in the previous section, the order of spaces does not suggest
an order of priority.

8.1 Competitive Pool

The competitive swim tank would provide space and opportunities not
currently available in Red Deer; namely, a high-level competition facility.
It would also provide for higher levels of synchronized swimming and
diving than is currently available in the city. However, it would be very
expensive to provide, both from an operating and a capital point of view.
It is unlikely that sources of funding from user groups, senior levels of
government, or the private sector would reduce the high costs significantly. Also, the new facility would severely and negatively impact the three
existing pools in the community, especially the Michner Centre. The
facility is somewhat flexible to serve varied uses, but its high proportion

of deep water reduces its flexibility and its fixed nature severely reduces its adaptability. Since what justifies the competition tank is competitions with spectators, and since accommodating up to 900 spectators for up to eight competitions per year (fifteen event days per year) is costly, the pool scores low on the participant vs. spectator scale. The relatively small number of participants in the competitive aquatics groups relative to the other larger, proven markets (e.g., soccer and tennis) reduce its economic viability and its breadth of access. The relatively high cost for members of these sports groups further reduces its breadth of access. Public demand is quite low (only 5%), certainly much lower than for the leisure aquatics facility.

The location of the proposed new recreation center for the 50M pool is not optimal. As a competition pool, it requires a warm-up and warm-down tank. It would be much more cost-effective to capitalize on the existence of such a tank at the recreation center, which already has much of the infrastructure (e.g., mechanical systems, warm up tank, area for a 50M tank, administration areas, dressing rooms, parking, and site services). In fact, developing a 50M tank at the site of the existing outdoor 50M tank at the recreation center in a central location in Red Deer would be much more cost-effective in the long run. Capital costs would be reduced by almost 30%, and the impact on the recreation center operating budget would be much less negative than if a 50M pool were developed on a separate site pulling uses away from the recreation center instead of adding uses.

8.2 Leisure Pool

Swimming for fun was one of the highest demands expressed in the public survey. A great many people want more such opportunities and feel that they are not currently provided in the city. The therapeutic nature of such a facility increases its utility and public value. However, the capital and operating costs are relatively high compared to other spaces (low compared to the competition pool) and the adaptability and flexibility are low.

8.3 Leisure Ice

Demand for leisure ice is high as shown in the public survey. It would also be a new opportunity which has not been available indoors in Red Deer before. It would be broadly accessible with no need to make a team, qualify at a given skill level, or join a club. It would be an excellent family-oriented activity. It is participant oriented by definition. The space would be somewhat flexible to use as a dry floor space and could be altered over time to serve another purpose, but not easily. Since there are no opportunities for skating in the immediate area, it would be a good location for such a facility. The capital costs are moderately high and the operating costs are also moderate.

8.4 Ice Arenas

There is some public demand for more arenas. However, they would do more to shift activity from other facilities than create new opportunities. They would replicate the existing ice sheets and generally provide more ice time to those that are already getting some. They are somewhat flexible and adaptable, but the specialized flooring would be wasted if put to a non-ice use. The location is good for a new ice facility as the existing facilities are not particularly close by.

8.5 Multipurpose Fieldhouse

This is the most demanded of all facilities in the public survey. It would provide a new opportunity not yet available in Red Deer, and as such, would serve those who are not being served in other indoor facilities. It is, by definition, a flexible space, capable of being configured to different kinds of use in the same week. It could also be adapted over time to serve other uses. It is expensive to build but very economical to operate, requiring little or no public subsidy. The location is ideal because the two high schools believe this is the one type of facility which they would want to use the most. It would serve some of the fastest-growing activities in Red Deer.

8.6 Gymnastics Gym

Although this facility did not score high on the public survey, gymnastics is a basic skill for young people and would serve a broad range of interests at least at the beginning level. With a high quality facility, it could become as popular as swimming, with most young people developing basic proficiency in the sport. Except for the cost of club membership (not necessarily a requirement for using the space), the facility would be quite broadly accessible. It is also quite economic, with little or no requirement for public subsidy to help build or operate the facility. The location is ideal given that both high schools have expressed an interest in the club contracting to supply facilities and instruction to high school students.

8.7 Preschool Program Areas

There was significant support for preschool spaces in the public survey. Most people see this as a logical part of a comprehensive public recreation complex. It is also something the Gymnastics Club sees as crucial to its operating success. Although there are many such spaces in the City, there are none in the southeast part of the city, so this element works well on this site. The space is not particularly flexible or adaptive but is quite cost-effective.

8.8 Multipurpose Areas

There is little public demand expressed for multipurpose spaces in the survey. However, if built, they would serve a broad cross-section of the public in a wide variety of ways. They would be generally quite accessible and relatively inexpensive for users to use. They are, by definition, very flexible in use and adaptable over time to other uses. They are also very cost-effective to build and operate. Although many similar spaces exist in the adjacent schools, and this lowers evaluation of such space on the optimization of location scale, the spaces in the schools are not always available when needed and not configured or equipped for public uses. There are many other such spaces in the city, so they are positioned to provide more of what is already being provided.

8.9 Swing Center

There is no test of public demand for this space, as it was conceived after the public survey and is not a standard facility type that would be easily recognized by the general public. It would, however, meet a different set of needs than have been met to date and would serve a broad cross-section of the public in a flexible and adaptable format. The space would be quite cost-effective in its low requirement of finished space. Most of the potential uses are growing in popularity and should continue to do so.

8.10 Retail Space

There is no real need to prioritize retail space. It could be left up to the private sector to determine if it is viable. If it is, there is no public subsidy required, merely the potential of net operating revenues to contribute to the complex operation. If it isn't viable, it won't happen.

8.11 Food and Beverage Space

Also, there is no need to prioritize the food and beverage space. A modest amount of food and beverage area will likely be developed to support whatever else gets built. If more spaces are included in the complex, there is likely need for more food and beverage service. It is a relatively small capital investment with little or no risk of a requirement for public subsidy.

The above discussion is summarized in Figure 18. Although readers should understand that this analysis is subjective, it is not arbitrary. In other words, the consultants believe that if a random sample of 100 Red Deer citizens were given the same evaluation criteria and the same background information, they would likely come to the same or similar scores. The scores are on a 3-point scale where a high score is given a value of 3, a moderate score a value of 2, and low score a value of 1. The scores are added to provide a numerical representation of this subjective process.

According to the results of the analysis as summarized in Figure 18, the highest priority for new spaces is for a multipurpose fieldhouse. It is followed closely by a swing center, leisure ice, a preschool program area, a leisure pool, a gymnastics gym, and multipurpose spaces. The two lowest priorities currently in Red Deer are new arenas and a competition pool. However, the leisure ice is tied closely to the arenas in terms of functionality, given that the operating costs would increase significantly if leisure ice were built without the arenas. Also, the competition pool, regardless of priority, would be better located on another site.

Component \ Evaluation Criteria	Public Demand	Community Benefit	Broad-Based Access	Participant Oriented vs. Spectator Oriented	Serving Expanding Needs	Variety Over Quantity	Adaptable and Flexible	Cost-Effective (Capital and Operating)	Optimization of Location	Priority Value
Competition Pool	Low	Mod	Mod	Mod	Low	Mod	Low	Low	Low	13
Leisure Pool	Hi	Mod	Hi	Hi	Mod	Mod	Low	Mod	Hi	21
Leisure Ice	Hi	Mod	Mod	Hi	Hi	Mod	Mod	Mod	Hi	22
Ice Arenas	Mod	Mod	Mod	Mod	Low	Low	Low	Mod	Hi	16
Multipurpose Fieldhouse	Hi	Mod	Hi	Hi	Hi	Hi	Hi	Hi	Mod	25
Gymnastics Gym	Low	Mod	Mod	Hi	Mod	Hi	Mod	Hi	Mod	20
Preschool Area	Mod	Mod	Hi	Hi	Mod	Mod	Mod	Hi	Hi	22
Multipurpose Areas	Low	Mod	Hi	Hi	Mod	Low	Hi	Hi	Mod	20
Swing Center	Low	Mod	Mod	Hi	Hi	Hi	Hi	Hi	Hi	23

Figure 18 Summary of Analysis of Facility, Component Scored Against Evaluation Criteria

APPENDIX D

Site Selection Process—A Case Study

Site Selection-Case Study

1. Introduction

The critical factor in marketing and generating use of any facility is location. This is due to a number of factors, some of which include:

- access and convenience
- visual prominence
- competition with similar facilities
- potential user population
- demographic profile of catchment area users
- adjacent amenities

The Winnipeg Physical Fitness Institute, Inc. recognized this fact when they first considered the development of a downtown fitness center. One of the primary objectives of the Institute was to locate the fitness center within a 5-minute walk of the corner of Portage Avenue and Main Street. While this factor was an important element in the development of the center, there were other factors that would have an important effect on the desirability and feasibility of developing the fitness center.

This section outlines the criteria and procedure used to evaluate all of the potential sites and recommends the sites most suitable for the development of a fitness center in the downtown area of Winnipeg.

2. Site Selection Procedure

There are many factors influencing the location of a fitness center. For the purposes of this study, a priority ranking system was developed to analytically assess the merits of each of the proposed sites.

The procedure consisted of:

1. Identifying the evaluative criteria to apply to each site

2. Weighting each of the criteria from 0.5-2.0 on the basis of the importance of each criterion

3. Identifying and describing each of the sites

4. Numerically rating each site against each of the criteria

5. Calculating the rating x weighting to establish the combined ranking (score) for each site

6. Analysis and ranking of sites on a priority basis

It is important to point out that this exercise is still somewhat sub-jective. However, it does allow for critical analysis of the sites and estab-lishes the "relative" merits of one site vs. each other site.

3. Site Selection Criteria

The following criteria were considered to be the most critical factors to consider in deciding on the location of the fitness center. It must be recog-nized that while some of the factors are more important than others, they all have relative importance to the overall potential success of the facility. For example, if a site were offered free, it would likely move to the top of the priority list. However, if the location was so far removed from the primary target market that it would be inconvenient to use, then it would likely receive a lower rating. The impact of each factor must be weighed on an individual basis.

3.1 Proximity to Portage Avenue and Main Street

Participation in fitness activities is governed by many factors as well. In recent years, through the efforts of ParticipACTION, fitness has be-come part of the lifestyle of many Canadians and is such a high priority that they overlook almost any obstacle to participate. For many others, however, any inconvenience would make it less likely that they would participate. Proximity to the workplace was seen as an important factor in influencing potential membership, frequency of visits, and intensity of use.

There are approximately 60,000 workers in the downtown area of the City of Winnipeg. It is estimated that close to 40,000 of these work-ers are within a 5-minute walk of the corner of Portage Avenue and Main Street. For persons interested in working out before or after work or at noon, it is critical that a minimum amount of time is wasted getting to the location. This was one of the reasons that the institute felt so strongly about locating the facility in this area.

For the corner of Portage and Main, a 5-minute walk west down Portage would end at Hargrave, and a 10-minute walk would end at Col-ony Street. The walkway system would take slightly longer. The map on the following page outlines the areas included within a 5- and 10-minute radius of the corner of Portage Avenue and Main Street.

3.2 Cost of the Land

In the downtown, there are very few available pieces of property and land costs are high. To acquire a suitable site, several options exist:

- Purchase a vacant property and build a stand-alone facility
- Lease land from a current landowner and develop a stand-alone facility
- Integrate the fitness center into plans for a new development currently under consideration (T. D. Tower)

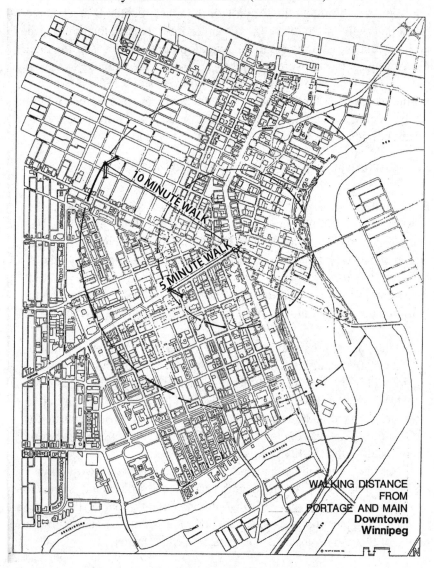

WALKING DISTANCE
FROM
PORTAGE AND MAIN
**Downtown
Winnipeg**

- Accept gift of land within public ownership (Forks, City)
- Have private landowner/developer construct facility and lease the space from the developer (ex. 129 McDermot)

Each of these options has varying advantages and disadvantages. They each have a different cost factor to consider as well. Free land in the wrong location would not be as beneficial as leased land in exactly the right location. Other "strings" would have to be considered as well before a decision was made. Many developers and landowners may have standards and regulations for use that make the development less attractive or more costly in the long run.

3.3 Ownership/Availability

This issue relates to the timeline for potential development. In some cases, that means sites considered in this evaluation exercise would take several years to negotiate. In other cases, a joint development might be slowed down by the timeline of the developer who may not want to begin construction for several years.

In either case, the site might prove less attractive simply because it would not be available in a reasonable time period. Even if other factors such as cost, location, and access were suitable, a site might receive a lower rating because of the delay in development.

3.4 Size of the Site

The size of the site is a critical factor. It is important to locate a site that can accommodate the proposed building program rather than compromising the building program to fit a particular site.

The fitness center has several large components that could make it difficult to incorporate within new office high-rise developments. These developments generally have a 30,000–35,000 square foot floor plate which could prove limiting. In addition, the size of site necessary to accommodate a stand-alone facility of this type in the downtown area could make the land costs prohibitive or simply not available.

3.5 Access

An important criterion closely related to location is access. There are several types of access which all must be considered in the location chosen for the fitness center. Perhaps the most important is public walking access to the site. It would be desirable to locate the facility on or adjacent to the concourse and walkway system so that the majority of daytime users would not have to put on heavy clothing during inclement weather.

It would also be important to have a location which was in close proximity to public transportation systems, had ample public parking nearby, could be easily reached by service and emergency vehicles, and was completely accessible for disabled persons wanting to use the center.

3.6 Aesthetics

The aesthetics of the surroundings applies as much to the area around the center as it does to the center itself. The visual appearance and environmental condition of the surrounding area influences the quality of the experience of the user. If participants have to walk through dark, dangerous areas or pass by unpleasant buildings and conditions, the quality of their experience is affected.

The aesthetic condition of the site relates to visual conditions and views, vegetation, smells, light, orientation of the building, and surrounding architecture.

3.7 Proximity to Complimentary or Competing Facilities

If the site chosen is adjacent to other facilities that complement a fitness center, then it is likely that participation and memberships will increase due to a "spin off" effect. If the center were located adjacent to a competing facility, participants would have to make a choice between two similar facilities and therefore divide the market potential of each facility. This would be both impractical and inadvisable.

3.8 Site Constraints

There are many site conditions and constraints that could affect the cost, availability, feasibility, and desirability of development.

Site constraints could include:

- existing development (removal, renovation, or retrofitting)
- zoning limitations
- servicing requirements
- parking regulations
- height restrictions
- architectural and environmental controls

3.9 Development Cost and Difficulty

Each site has varying potential for development based on many of the factors outlined above. Zoning affects the cost of development as does location, access, site conditions, and controls.

It may be more cost-effective to build a new facility than to attempt to renovate an older building, particularly if it has a heritage designation. It may also be more cost-effective to construct a new stand-alone facility than to incorporate it into another proposed new development.

4. Weighting the Site Selection Criteria

Criteria	Weight
1. Cost of Land	1.0
2. Ownership /Availability	1.5
3. Size of Site	0.5
4. Access	0.5
5. Aesthetics	0.5
6. Proximity to Comp. Fac.	0.5
7. Site Constraints	0.5
8. Development Costs	1.0
9. Proximity Portage/Main	2.0

Table 1. Weight of Site Criteria

The next task was to determine the criteria that were most important and, therefore, should receive a greater weight. This was done by first considering the goals of the Institute and the expectations of the site. It was also important to consider which of the factors or criteria would have the greatest effect and impact on the desirability and feasibility of proceeding with the development.

It was determined that the most important factors to consider, in priority order, were:

1. Proximity to Portage Avenue and Main Street

2. Availability of the property

3. Cost (to purchase, lease, and/or develop)

4. Practicality / Feasibility

Any of the site criteria or factors that fell into the four areas listed above was assigned a numerical weight accordingly. The weights assigned to each criteria are illustrated in Table 1.

5. Description of Proposed Sites

Following are the eight sites that appeared to represent the most feasible locations. Please see the map on the following page to locate each of the sites. Sites numbered 7 and 8 were not reviewed in detail as there are serious restrictions to the development of these sites.

5.1 North Portage (Site Option #1)

The North Portage location represents the most removed site from the corner of Portage Avenue and Main Street and would be in close proximity to the Y.M./Y.W.C.A site should it proceed. It would, however, be available at little or no cost, be located directly on the walkway system, and have ample public parking (1000 cars) available. The location is presently owned by the North Portage Development Corporation, and the site in mind would be one of the two towers planned for development at opposite ends of the current complex.

   The land would be available on a leased basis, but development would be governed by current site and architectural standards. The amount and configuration of the space available (30,000–35,000 sq. ft.) would create some constraints and require some compromise to the proposed building program.

5.2 Silpit Industries (Site Option #2)

The Silpit site, located at 70 Arthur Street, is owned by Silpit Industries and has an old building on the site that would lend itself to renovation or retrofitting. The advantages of the site are that the lease cost would be reasonable, and the owners are interested and willing to look at a proposal to develop the space as a fitness center.

   The problems with the site are that it is removed from the walkway system and the corner of Portage and Main Street, access is difficult, the site is not aesthetically appealing, and it would require considerable compromise to the building program and extensive renovations to make the facilities fit in the space available.

5.3 Lincor Properties Ltd. (Site Option # 3)

The Lincor site located at 225 Graham Ave. is to be developed as an office tower with the potential to add space for the fitness center. The location is excellent and in close proximity to the corner of Portage and Main

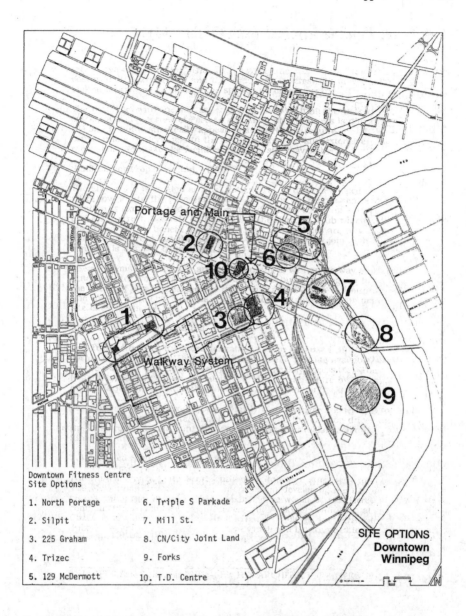

Downtown Fitness Centre
Site Options

1. North Portage
2. Silpit
3. 225 Graham
4. Trizec
5. 129 McDermott
6. Triple S Parkade
7. Mill St.
8. CN/City Joint Land
9. Forks
10. T.D. Centre

SITE OPTIONS
Downtown Winnipeg

Street. It would be adjacent to the Carleton Club that might be either a benefit or a liability. The two facilities are very different in nature, but the number of people who might join both facilities is difficult to estimate.

The problems with the site are that planning is well on its way, and the fitness center would have to compromise the building program to fit the site as it is a standard office tower with a 30,000 sq. ft. footprint. The cost to lease space at this site would be high, and there are many site constraints.

5.4 Trizec Equities Limited (Site Option #4)

The Trizec site is at the most desirable location because it is at the corner of Portage and Main Street, has excellent parking available, is on the walkway and concourse system, and is easily accessible. There is some precedent for the development of a fitness center by Trizec, as such a facility was built in the Bankers Hall Building in Calgary.

The costs at this site would be extremely high as there are services to move, the roof on the site must be stripped, and the location drives up the lease costs. In addition, the owners are not enthusiastic about a fitness center at the site.

5.5 United Equities (129 McDermot Site Option #5)

The United Equities site is presently an outdoor parking lot located at 129 McDermot. The owners are interested in developing the site for offices, retail, and parking, and a fitness center would be considered a complementary facility. It is adjacent to the walkway connection at the Chamber of Commerce and Grain Exchange buildings and overlooks Juba Park and the Forks Trail system that was extended to the Legislative Buildings in the summer of 1990.

The site is of a suitable size to allow for development of all proposed components of the fitness center. It has good access and is reasonably close to the corner of Portage and Main. There are few site constraints and is perhaps the most aesthetically pleasing site.

This site represents one of the best alternatives in that the owner is willing to construct the building and lease the space on a long-term basis. The leasehold improvements would be made by the fitness center, thereby reducing the capital commitment of the owners and reducing the overall lease cost.

5.6 Triple S Parking (Site Option #6)

The site is located adjacent to the Chamber of Commerce and Grain Exchange buildings between Lombard and McDermot. The site has good access, close proximity to Portage and Main, and is an undeveloped parking lot at present.

There is a proposal to construct an indoor parking structure on the site in the near future, but the time line is unclear. It would be possible to include a fitness center as a component of the development, but the site is very small, and compromises to the building program would be necessary and development may be delayed for some time.

5.7 *The Forks (Site Option #9)*

The Forks site is removed from the corner of Portage and Main and is a long way from the walkway system. It does, however, have available, undeveloped land with minimal site constraints. It is aesthetically the most pleasing site with many adjacent complimentary facilities, and the land could be available at little or no charge.

The problem with the site is the location, access, and development costs for the site.

5.8 *Toronto Dominion Centre (Site Option #10)*

The T. D. Centre is also located at the corner of Portage and Main and would have excellent access and be close to complementary facilities.

The problems with the site are the cost to develop a facility in the proposed second office tower, the amount of space available, the site constraints, and the schedule for eventual development of the tower.

6. Analysis and Ranking of Each Site

The first step in this procedure was to assign a value from 1 to 10 to each of the criteria for each of the sites. After this was completed, each of the site criteria was multiplied by the weighting it had received earlier and the composite score calculated. A summary of the site analysis and ranking appears in Table 2. (Please note, the site numbers in Table 2 do not correspond with the map numbers, as Site numbers 7 and 8, while noted on the map, were not included in the site analysis.)

Based on the analysis of all of the potential sites, the most desirable, in priority order, are the United Equities property on McDermot, Triple S, and The Forks. It should be pointed out that each of these sites has limitations, some of which appear to be insurmountable. The approach to site acquisition and development is to begin negotiations with several of the priority sites to determine which will offer the best financial opportunities. If none of the top sites are available, there are other locations that while they represent a fall back position, are nonetheless worthy of pursuing.

At present, the site that has the best potential for development is United Equities at 129 McDermot. Preliminary discussions with the prop-

Criteria	Weight	1 North Portage	2 Silpit	3 225 Graham	4 Trizec	5 129 McDermot	6 Triple S Parking	7 The Forks	8 T.D. Centre
Cost of Land	1.0	10	8	3	3	6	6	10	3
Ownership/Availability	1.5	15	7.5	6	1.5	12	10.5	7.5	6
Size	.5	3.5	2	2.5	2.5	4	2	5	2.5
Access (bus, auto, walkway)	.5	3	2	4	4.5	2.5	2.5	3	4.5
Aesthetics	.5	3	2	3	3	4.5	2	5	3
Relationship to Comp. Facilities	.5	4	2	3.5	3.5	4	3.5	4.5	3.5
Site Constraints	.5	3.5	2.5	2	2.5	3.5	2	5	2
Development Cost	1.0	7	3	5	4	8	8	6	4
Proximity to Portage & Main	2.0	2	10	16	18	12	14	4	20
Total		51	41.5	48.5	46	60.5	54.5	51.5	52
Rank/Priority		5	8	6	7	1	2	4	3

Table 2 Site Selection Composite Rating

erty owner indicated an interest in jointly developing the fitness center on this property. The Winnipeg Physical Fitness Institute should follow up discussions with United Equities if a decision is made to proceed with the development of the fitness center.

Other

There were several other sites considered for development of the fitness center. Many of the sites were deemed to be impractical at the present time because of other proposed developments at that location or other limiting factors such as location, cost, and existing development. Included among these facilities were:

- Federal Government Customs Building
- Grain Exchange Building
- Mill Street, City property
- CN/City Joint Lands
- Amy Street Power Plant
- Hotel Development at North Portage
- Winnipeg Free Press site
- Winnipeg Tribune site
- South Portage
- Bank of Commerce Building

Other Books by Venture Publishing, Inc.

21st Century Leisure: Current Issues, Second Edition
    by Valeria J. Freysinger and John R. Kelly
The A•B•Cs of Behavior Change: Skills for Working With Behavior Problems in Nursing Homes
    by Margaret D. Cohn, Michael A. Smyer, and Ann L. Horgas
Activity Experiences and Programming within Long-Term Care
    by Ted Tedrick and Elaine R. Green
The Activity Gourmet
    by Peggy Powers
Advanced Concepts for Geriatric Nursing Assistants
    by Carolyn A. McDonald
Adventure Programming
    edited by John C. Miles and Simon Priest
Assessment: The Cornerstone of Activity Programs
    by Ruth Perschbacher
Behavior Modification in Therapeutic Recreation: An Introductory Manual
    by John Datillo and William D. Murphy
Benefits of Leisure
    edited by B.L. Driver, Perry J. Brown, and George L. Peterson
Benefits of Recreation Research Update
    by Judy M. Sefton and W. Kerry Mummery
Beyond Baskets and Beads: Activities for Older Adults with Functional Impairments
    by Mary Hart, Karen Primm, and Kathy Cranisky
Beyond Bingo: Innovative Programs for the New Senior
    by Sal Arrigo, Jr., Ann Lewis, and Hank Mattimore
Beyond Bingo 2: More Innovative Programs for the New Senior
    by Sal Arrigo, Jr.
Boredom Busters: Themed Special Events to Dazzle and Delight Your Group
    by Annette C. Moore
Both Gains and Gaps: Feminist Perspectives on Women's Leisure
    by Karla Henderson, M. Deborah Bialeschki, Susan M. Shaw, and Valeria J. Freysinger
Brain Fitness
    by Suzanne Fitzsimmons
Client Assessment in Therapeutic Recreation Services
    by Norma J. Stumbo

Great Special Events and Activities
    by Annie Morton, Angie Prosser, and Sue Spangler
Group Games & Activity Leadership
    by Kenneth J. Bulik
Growing With Care: Using Greenery, Gardens, and Nature With Aging and Special Populations
    by Betsy Kreidler
Hands On! Children's Activities for Fairs, Festivals, and Special Events
    by Karen L. Ramey
Health Promotion for Mind, Body and Spirit
    by Suzanne Fitzsimmons and Linda L. Buettner
In Search of the Starfish: Creating a Caring Environment
    by Mary Hart, Karen Primm, and Kathy Cranisky
Inclusion: Including People With Disabilities in Parks and Recreation Opportunities
    by Lynn Anderson and Carla Brown Kress
Inclusive Leisure Services: Responding to the Rights of People with Disabilities, Second Edition
    by John Dattilo
Innovations: A Recreation Therapy Approach to Restorative Programs
    by Dawn R. De Vries and Julie M. Lake
Internships in Recreation and Leisure Services: A Practical Guide for Students, Fourth Edition
    by Edward E. Seagle, Jr. and Ralph W. Smith
Interpretation of Cultural and Natural Resources, Second Edition
    by Douglas M. Knudson, Ted T. Cable, and Larry Beck
Intervention Activities for At-Risk Youth
    by Norma J. Stumbo
Introduction to Outdoor Recreation: Providing and Managing Resource Based Opportunities
    by Roger L. Moore and B.L. Driver
Introduction to Recreation and Leisure Services, Eighth Edition
    by Karla A. Henderson, M. Deborah Bialeschki, John L. Hemingway, Jan S. Hodges, Beth D. Kivel, and H. Douglas Sessoms
Introduction to Therapeutic Recreation: U.S. and Canadian Perspectives
    by Kenneth Mobily and Lisa Ostiguy
Introduction to Writing Goals and Objectives: A Manual for Recreation Therapy Students and Entry-Level Professionals
    by Suzanne Melcher

Therapeutic Recreation in the Nursing Home
    by Linda Buettner and Shelley L. Martin
Therapeutic Recreation Programming: Theory and Practice
    by Charles Sylvester, Judith E. Voelkl, and Gary D. Ellis
Therapeutic Recreation Protocol for Treatment of Substance Addictions
    by Rozanne W. Faulkner
The Therapeutic Recreation Stress Management Primer
    by Cynthia Mascott
The Therapeutic Value of Creative Writing
    by Paul M. Spicer
Tourism and Society: A Guide to Problems and Issues
    by Robert W. Wyllie
Traditions: Improving Quality of Life in Caregiving
    by Janelle Sellick
Trivia by the Dozen: Encouraging Interaction and Reminiscence in Managed Care
    by Jean Vetter